THE RED BOOK

OF HOUSTON

A Compendium of
Social, Professional, Religious, Educational and Industrial Interests
of Houston's Colored Population

EDITION NUMBER ONE

PRICE

$3.50

PUBLISHED BY

SOTEX PUBLISHING COMPANY

HOUSTON, TEXAS

CUMMING & SONS, ART PRINTERS HOUSTON

Introductory

In placing the RED BOOK before the public it is not the intention of the publishers to color, to flatter or to cover any fact or condition, or to take into consideration any of the so-called racial problems, or to unduly advertise any race or man, or to draw any comparisons, or to make any bid for notoriety or publicity, but merely to give credit where credit is due and to set down in permanent form the record of some of the members of the African race who stand for the uplift. It is a compilation of the facts and conditions socially, religiously, educationally, professionally and industrially drawn from the lives and work of those who stand for better things for the race.

The paths of racial peace are straight and narrow.

The Ruler of the Universe has designed that some skins be black, some white, some yellow, some brown, some red. Still the color of the skin does not always determine the characteristics. The only way we can determine that is by the life led by the race.

Every individual owes it to his race to remain true to the racial lines and traditions and to work up, through the mediums offered, to the best life possible under the conditions.

Despite the existence of a few critics, carpers and cranks, racial prejudices between the white and black races in the South are dying out. No longer does either race desire to carry or be carried on the back of the other.

A sane readjustment of racial differences, a sensible view of racial incompatibilities and a practical knowledge of racial characteristics, such as we now have, is taking the sting of contact away and good feeling in the main is manifested between the two races, geographically together but racially far apart.

It is a well known fact that the feeling of Racial Pride now has a greater hold on the sentiments of the Afro-American race than ever before in its history.

The Afro-American knows and has always known that the prosperity of the white race has always meant his prosperity and the common-sense element of the white race is learning fast that the progress and prosperity of the Afro-American race is good for both races.

Despite the carpers of both races, the Afro-American race fares better among the whites of the Southern States than anywhere else in the world.

A careful analysis of the progress of those of the race, who are surrounded by suitable conditions and have proper encouragement, shows that since the Civil War, it has surpassed that of any known race that has come up out of slavery.

Each race, and especially the Afro-American, has found that greater advancement is to be made along rational, racial lines, and greater profit and pleasure comes from adhering strictly to these.

A worthy man in his race, whatever it is, loses that worthiness when he attempts to obliterate social and racial barriers imposed by a beneficent Jehovah. He must stay in his own to prove the worthiness of his life.

So simply with a desire to give true inspiration through the medium of a permanent record of achievement to those of the race who appreciate its value and with the knowledge that every man is entitled to due credit, no matter the race, the state or condition, this book is dedicated to those who stand for the uplift, with the hope that it will hurt no man but be of large benefit to many and many more yet to come.

THE PUBLISHERS.

A FEW HARRIS COUNTY SURVIVORS OF ANTE-BELLUM DAYS.

Left to Right, Name and Ages. Standing: Tommy Robinson 88, John Butler, 72, Anti. Robinson, Aaron Thompson, 102; Ben Moore, 65; Roe Cornelius, 71; James Seward, 70; Henry Williams Seated: Wash. Williams, 75; Martha Antonct Roberts Lawrence, 80; Sam Teran, 124; Bob Holmes, 116; Manly Harris, 93; Cato Roberts, 94; Melvin Williams, 59; Viola Wallace, 80.

HARRIS STUDIO
CITY 1-2-1915

THE AUTHOR

EFFICIENCY

By EMMETT J. SCOTT

EXECUTIVE SECRETARY TUSKEGEE NORMAL AND
INDUSTRIAL INSTITUTE

In our educational life, in our industrial life, in most of our efforts and strivings, the Negro is now face to face with new conditions. Circumstances have landed him, all unprepared, as it were, into the midst of the keenest struggle for survival that is taking place anywhere in the world.

Education is the means through which we, the Negro people, are to be prepared to meet these changing conditions and survive in this competition. The whole method of modern education is inspired with a desire to equip its students for life, to make them, in short, efficient.

We have heard a great deal of discussion in recent years about the value of different kinds of education. I hazard the statement that in all the world there are, despite angry contention and futile discussion to the contrary, but two kinds of education—the "efficient" and the "inefficient." The education which first of all helps a man to find himself and the powers that are within him, and next to use these trained powers in service for his fellows is efficient education, and the education which fails to do this is inefficient education.

The first strivings of the race following emancipation were to acquire the education of the traditional curriculum without considering whether it had reference to the things of life or not.

During the first fifty years of freedom we, as a race, have been mainly interested in proving to ourselves and to the world that we could swallow and digest, at least sufficiently to meet the requirements of the schools, just as much of the material in books as any other race.

The time has now come, however, when the Negro race must, as Prof. Kelly Miller says: "Transmute those figurative substances into power." That means that as a race we have got "to get busy," to show what we can do with the education we have acquired beside merely handing it down as a tradition to others.

What does that mean? It means that no school, anywhere in the land, shall, in the future, be counted only so far as it is able to make itself felt in the every-day life of those whom it is designed to serve. The time has come for us everywhere, in our education and in our daily activities, to seek to supply our own needs and take advantage of our economic opportunities.

What are some of these needs and opportunities? First of all, we need to acquire the habit of reading books. In slavery the Negro made the acquaintance of the English language, which, to quote Prof. Miller again, is "the most effective agency of civilization now operating on the face of the earth." In the first fifty years after slavery we have learned, to a very large extent, the technique, the formal elements of reading and writing. We have in our possession the secrets of all the knowledge and culture of the world. But to what extent have we made use of that knowledge? How many of us make use in our daily life of the vast stores of information upon every conceivable subject which are to be found in current literature, in the magazines and books that are daily issuing from the press? How many of our teachers or students keep track even of the events of vital interest to our race that are transpiring every day?

How many of our people, for instance, know anything at all about the organization and the work of the Stokes Fund, which has its investigators looking into the whole subject of Negro education in the South, inspecting Negro institutions of learning to determine their elements of strength and weakness, of the Anna T Jeanes Fund, which is helping the rural schools for Negroes by providing teachers and supervisors and directing their work along sane and progressive lines, of the Southern Sociological Congress, that body of intelligent Southerners who meet annually and whose sole purpose is to work out a program of race adjustment, fair alike to blacks and whites, of the University Commission, composed of representatives of each of the great universities of the South, for the study of the race question, of Prof William I Thomas, of the University of Chicago, and of his study of the peasants in Europe, and who has shown how closely akin the problems of the peasant in Europe are to those of the Negro in America? How many of our people know anything at all of the workings of these organizations and agencies which are setting in motion forces of incalculable value to us as a race?

To bring the question nearer home to you, let me ask, how many of our people who live in Texas actually know about conditions in their own State, in their own counties?

One of the problems that deserves our earnest attention is health conditions among our people throughout the land These facts developed at a recent Health Conference on the Negro are almost startling

450,000 Negroes in the South are seriously ill all the time this means 18 days a year for each Negro inhabitant in the South

The annual cost of the sickness of these 450,000 Negroes is $75,000,000

112 000 Negro workers in the South are sick all the time, their annual loss in earnings is $45,000 000

45 per cent of the annual deaths among the Negroes of the South are preventable

225,000 Negroes in the South die annually, and it is estimated that 100,000 of these could be prevented

600,000 Negroes of the present population will die from tuberculosis, 150,000 of these can and should be saved.

The annual funeral expenses of Negroes in the South amount to $15 000,000, $6,500,-000 of this sum could be saved

The annual loss to the South in potential earnings because of preventable deaths among Negroes is $170,000 000

Sickness and deaths cost our people in the South $100,000,000 annually and $50,000 -000 of this amount could be saved

These facts have been compiled by Mr Monroe N Work, a statistician of proved ability, and I am sure they may be trusted as being absolutely true

But let me bring these statements nearer home There are each year among the colored people of Houston probably from 700 to 800 deaths About 45 per cent of these deaths are preventable, that is, over 300 of our people die each year in Houston whose lives could be saved There are in the City of Houston some 30,000 colored people According to vital statistics about 1,500 of these colored people are seriously ill all the time, and the annual loss in earnings of these sick persons amounts to some $180,000 The doctors' bills among the colored people of Houston amount to about $250,000 per year, while the funeral expenses among our people in Houston amount to about $40,000 per year The value of the lives of the 300 people who might have been prevented from dying, according to the average value of man's life, was about $510,000, and the total annual loss to the City of Houston through the sickness and death of our people is about $1,000,000

Texas claims, and rightly, that she has the best schools for Negroes in the country The schools of Houston lead the State Let me urge that through these schools the fundamental lessons of good health be taught, not only to the pupils but also to the people at large No school should count itself doing its best unless it turn its attention to saving lives, in improving the health of the people, and in helping them in these vital and particular directions

These are facts which our teachers should be familiar with, they are facts that should be taught in the schools in connection with hygiene The school should be the agency for distributing these facts among our people

We must study in the schools not merely the formal matters in the text-books, but we must connect these matters with those matters of special import and interest to our people

In the country at large 87 per cent of Negro males are engaged in gainful pursuits 54 per cent or more of the females of our race are similarly engaged in the gainful pursuits Of the whites, 78 per cent of the males are so engaged, and only 18 per cent of white females What does this mean? If it means anything at all, it means that the Negroes in the United States are engaged primarily in the basic, fundamental industries What will help to quicken the industrial intelligence of this group of men and women will raise the whole level of life among our people and bring into operation forces of extraordinary power and might

Now, the fact which I want to impress upon the young men and women who have the superior advantages offered by the schools of Texas is the manner in which they and all of us are dependent upon the progress of the masses of the people

Mr Clarence H Poe, himself a Southerner, has stated this fact with startling clearness, in a discussion of the Negro's relation to Southern prosperity Said he

"I do not know whether or not it has ever worked out as a principle of political economy, but it is unquestionably true that wealth is by nature not aristocratic, but democratic The poorer every other man is, the poorer you are The richer every other man is, the richer you are Every man whose earning power is below par, below normal, is a burden on the community, he drags down the whole level of life, and every other man in the community is poorer by reason of his presence, whether he be white man or Negro or what not Your untrained, inefficient man is not only a poverty-breeder for himself, but the contagion of it curses every man in the community that is guilty of leaving him untrained The law of changeless justice decrees that you must rise or fall, decline or prosper, with your neighbor You will be richer for his wealth, poorer for his poverty So today every man in the South who is tilling an acre of land so that it produces only half as much as intelligently directed labor would get out of it is a burden on the community Suppose you are his fellow citizen, then, because of his inefficiency his poverty because of his failure to contribute to public funds and public movements, you must have poorer roads, poorer schools, a meaner school house and court house, a shabbier church, lower priced lands, your teacher will be more poorly paid your preacher's salary will be smaller your newspaper will have a smaller circulation, your town will have a poorer market, your railroad smaller traffic, your merchant smaller trade, your bank smaller deposits, your manufacturer diminished patronage, and so on, and so on The ramifications are infinite, unending The doctrine is true whatever the color of the man Let us remember then that our economic law knows no color line White or black the man whose efficiency is above par, economically considered, is a help, white or black, the man whose efficiency is below par is a hindrance"

It is incumbent upon us, every one of us, then, to help reach the unreached" of our race, not only in their moral helping, but in their industrial helping, as well for what lifts one Negro lifts all, and what retards one retards all With us, the call is to establish on an enduring foundation not only the intelligence of our race, but its industrial efficiency as well In agriculture, in the trades, in domestic life in the professions, in all the vocations, our economic status is to be improved if we would not be crowded to the wall by the keen competitions of American life And in our struggle we shall continue to receive as we have always received the sympathetic support of the strongest forces in our Southern life

Some time ago Dr Washington, speaking at Philadelphia, gave utterance to some important statements In admonishing the Negro people of the United States of their advantages and opportunities, he pointed out that in the South alone among us, "a nation within a nation," 6,000 dry goods stores could be supported by Negroes alone, 4,500 drug stores could be supported by Negroes alone, 10,000 grocery stores could be supported by Negroes alone, 3,000 shoe stores could be supported by Negroes alone, 3,000 millinery stores could be supported by Negroes alone, 3,000 additional banks could be supported by Negroes alone, in other words if the nine million Negroes of the South were as progressive as alert, as willing to take advantage of their opportunities as they should be, they could easily and well support 30,000 additional stores and banks

But I wish to bring these facts closer home to you, men and women of Texas Based upon the population of this State, you should be in position to establish and creditably maintain not less than 200 dry goods stores You should be able to support not less than 500 grocery stores 100 millinery stores and 100 shoe stores   How many have you now? There ought to be in the State ten Negro banks

In the past ten or fifteen years land values in the South have increased very rapidly In some instances the increase has been from one hundred to five hundred per cent Lands which fifteen years ago were selling at from $2 50 to $15 00 per acre are now selling at from $20 00 to $100 00 per acre The wealth of the South has been increased by the rise in land values alone over $500 000 000

To what extent has the Negro of the South, to what extent has the Texas Negro, shared in these increased land values? 200,000,000 acres or over 50 per cent of the total land in the South is unimproved There are about 10,000,000 in Alabama, 9 000 000 in Arkansas, 12,000,000 in Georgia 5,000,000 in Louisiana, 6,000,000 in South Carolina and 85,000,000 acres in Texas that are unimproved

Texas is the State of opportunity for agricultural improvement There are in the State 112,000,000 acres of farm lands, of which only 27,000 000 acres have been improved, that is, actually being cultivated Of this vast domain Negroes own about 2,000 000 acres There are in the State 85,000,000 acres of unimproved farm lands This is an area equal to all the New England States, New York and Pennsylvania Here are opportunities for thousands of Negroes to secure land, to engage in farming in stock raising and thus to root themselves in the soil

If I might address the leaders among the Negro people of Texas, I would say You men who have been favored whether by circumstance or by your own efforts owe it to your less fortunate fellows to keep before them this one vital, throbbing fact a landless people is forever and a day the "sport of the gods," and without sober standing in the community Thoreau has written a line which should be engraved and placed above every black man's door   "If a man write a better book, preach a better sermon, or make a better basket than his neighbor, though he build his house in the woods, the world will make a beaten path to his door "

If we make ourselves permanently useful, we shall deserve, as we shall receive the encouragement and the support of those among whom we live "If a man make a better basket than his neighbor " even though he be black, the world will buy of him the baskets it needs!

Before concluding this article I wish to speak more definitely concerning the progress that the race has made in the past fifty years In doing so I shall quote at length from the Negro Year Book, that great source of information, of which I am one of the publishers, concerning what the Negro is doing The Year Book states· "Fifty years ago the education of the Negro in the South had just begun There were less than 100 schools devoted to this purpose In 1867 there were only 1,839 schools for the freedmen with 2,087 teachers, of whom 699 were colored There were 111,442 pupils 18,758 of these people were studying the alphabet 55,163 were in the spelling and easy reading lesson classes 42,879 were learning to write 40,454 were studying arithmetic 4,661 were studying the higher branches 35 industrial schools were reported, in which there were 2,124 students who were taught sewing, knitting, straw braiding, repairing and making garments In 1912-13 there are over 1,700,000 Negro children enrolled in the public schools of the South and over 100,000 in the normal schools and colleges The 699 colored teachers of 1867 have increased to over 34,000, of whom 3,000 are teachers in colleges, normal and industrial schools

In 1863 there were in the South no institutions for higher and secondary education of the Negro There were only four in the entire United States In 1914 there are in the South fifty colleges devoted to their training There are 13 institutions for the education of Negro women There are 26 theological schools and departments There are three schools of law five of medicine, two of dentistry, four of pharmacy 17 State agricultural and mechanical colleges, and over 400 normal and industrial schools

Fifty years ago the value of the school property used in the education of the freedmen was small The value of the property now owned by institutions for their secondary and higher training is over $17,000,000 Fifty years ago only a few thousand dollars were being expended for the education of the Negroes In 1914 over $4,100,000 was expended for their higher and industrial training and $9,700,000 in their public schools

Fifty years ago there were no funds specially devoted to the education of the Negroes Now there are eleven educational funds from which the Negro is deriving some assistance These are the "African Third,' the Avery, the John C Martin, the Miner, the Cushing, the Peabody, the John F Slater, the Daniel Hand, the Anna T Jeanes the Phelps-Stokes and the General Educational Board

Fifty years ago there were no national organizations among the Negroes There are now for their educational advancement the American Negro Academy, the National Association of Teachers in Colored Schools and the Negro National Educational Congress; for their economic advancement there are the National Negro Business League the National Bankers' Association and the National Association of Funeral Directors, for their professional advancement there are the National Medical Association the National Association of Colored Graduate Nurses, the National Negro Bar Association, the National Negro Press Association and the National Association of Colored Music and Art Clubs In the interest of Negro women there is the National Association of Colored Women's Clubs

Fifty years ago, with the exception of a few carpenters, blacksmiths and masons, practically all the Negroes in the South were agricultural workers Freedom gave them an opportunity to engage in all sorts of occupations The census reports show that there are now very few, if any, pursuits followed by whites in which there are not some Negroes There are over 50,000 in the professions, that is, teachers, preachers, lawyers, doctors dentists, editors etc There are some 40,000 engaged in business of various sorts

Fifty years ago there were in the South no Negro architects, electricians, photographers, druggists pharmacists, dentists, physicians, or surgeons no Negro owners of mines, cotton mills. dry goods stores, insurance companies, publishing houses or theatres, no wholesale merchants, no newspapers or editors, no undertakers, no real estate dealers, and no hospitals managed by Negroes Now there are Negroes managing all the above kinds of enterprises They are editing 450 newspapers and periodicals They own 100 insurance companies, 500 drug stores and over 20,000 grocery and other stores There are 500,000 or more Negroes working in the trades and in other occupations requiring skill blacksmiths, carpenters, cabinet makers, masons, miners, engineers, iron and steel workers, factory operators, printers, lithographers, engravers, gold and silver workers, tool and cutlery makers, etc

In 1863 it was not in the imagination of the most optimistic that within fifty years Negroes would be making good in the field of finance, be receiving ratings in the financial world, and be successful operators of banks When in 1888 the Legislature of Virginia was asked to grant a charter for a Negro bank, the request was at first treated as a joke There are now twelve Negro banks in that State and 57 in the entire country They are capitalized at about $1,600,000 They do an annual business of about $20,000,000

Great progress has been made in agriculture In 1863 there were in all the United States only a few farms controlled by Negroes They now operate in the South 890,140 farms, which are 217,800 more than there were in this section in 1863 Negro farm laborers and Negro farmers in the South now cultivate approximately 100,000,000 acres of land, of which 42,500,000 acres are under the control of Negro farmers

During the past fifty years there has been a rapid increase in the wealth of the Negroes of the South This increase was especially marked in the past ten years, during which time the value of the domestic animals which they own increased from $85,216,337 to $177,273,785, or 107 per cent, poultry from $3,788,792 to $5,113,756, or 35 per cent, implements and machinery from $18 586,225 to $36 861,418 or 98 per cent, land and buildings from $69,636,420 to $273,501,665, or 293 per cent From 1900 to 1910 the total value of farm property owned by the colored farmers of the South increased from $177,-404,688 to $492 898,218, or 177 per cent In 1863 the total wealth of the Negroes of this country was about $20,000,000 Now their total wealth is $700 000 000

No other emancipated people have made so great a progress in so short a time The Russian serfs were emancipated in 1861 Fifty years after it was found that 14,000,000 of them had accumulated about $500,000,000 worth of property or about $36 per capita, an average of about $200 per family Fifty years after their emancipation only about 30 per cent of the Russian peasants were able to read and write After fifty years of freedom the ten million Negroes in the United States have accumulated over $700,000,000 worth of property, or about $70 per capita, which is an average of $350 per family After fifty years of freedom 70 per cent of them have some education in books

This is an inspiring record, it is a record of which to be proud, but as great as has been the achievements of the past the work before us for the future will challenge our best endeavors of heart and brain, and we must enlist for a struggle which shall test whether or not the Negro is to survive or perish I believe he will survive, any other thought in the light of past accomplishments, with God's aid and guidance, is to me unthinkable   EMMETT J SCOTT

MEMORANDUM IN RE EMMETT J SCOTT, TUSKEGEE INSTITUTE, ALA

The author of this article, Emmett J Scott, is a former citizen of Texas, having been born and reared in Houston Since 1807 he has been employed consecutively as secretary to Dr Booker T Washington, the principal of Tuskegee Normal and Industrial Institute, Tuskegee, Alabama, and has during that time also been elected by the Board of Trustees as Executive Secretary of the Institute. He is also secretary of the National Negro Business League, and the official secretary of the International Conference on the Negro which was organized in April, 1912.

Of his services to Tuskegee Institute, Dr. Washington has written in his autobiography as follows: "Mr. Scott has served the school with rare fidelity and zeal, and has been to the principal not only a loyal assistant in every phase of his manifold and frequently trying duties, but has proven a valuable personal friend and counsellor in matters of the most delicate nature. * * * Only once or twice in a lifetime are such people discovered."

Of him, also, Dr. Robert E. Jones, editor of The Southwestern Christian Advocate, published in New Orleans, Louisiana, writes: "EMMETT J. SCOTT is the pride of Texas, an honored son of the whole race. He is a product of Wiley University, Marshall, Texas, and this distinguished alumnus of this Texas institution is loved and honored, not only by the Alumni of Wiley and the Methodist host of Texas and this Southland, but his friends and admirers are legion the country over. He was discovered by Dr. Booker T. Washington fourteen years ago, when he was in Houston, the editor of the Texas Freeman, which he had founded. Previous to this time Mr. Scott had done work upon the white dailies of Houston. Mr. Scott is best known as the Executive Secretary of the Tuskegee Institute and the strong right hand of Dr. Washington.

"He enjoys the full confidence of his chief, and because of Mr. Scott's clear thinking, devotion to high ideals, his integrity, and his high moral character, he has not only been able to serve Dr. Washington and the great Tuskegee Institute, but he has made a place of his own. It was no empty honor when President Taft appointed him one of three commissioners to the Republic of Liberia, being the first Negro ever sent abroad on a warship by our government on a like mission.

"Emmett J. Scott is a prince, a man of large capacity for work, of great poise, and deliberation in a very marked degree. He would be successful in anything that he would undertake. He is a member of our great Trinity Church in Houston, Texas, where he is held in the highest esteem. He is a prophet with honor in his own home as well as abroad."

COLORED CARNEGIE LIBRARY.

The Colored Carnegie Library was the outgrowth of the Library Association, which was organized in 1907 by Professor E. O. Smith. The school board allowed the use of a room in the Colored High School building for three years, during which time the City of Houston appropriated $500 for its maintenance. The association collected several hundreds of volumes and raised $500 in money among the colored people, with which a lot was purchased for a permanent site. In 1910 Mr. Andrew Carnegie appropriated $15,000 for a building, on condition that the city contribute 10 per cent annually for its upkeep. The library has 1500 readers and furnishes an excellent supplement to Houston's splendid school system. It has 3500 books. The trustees at the time the building was dedicated and whose names appear on the cornerstone, are E. O. Smith, pres.; J. B. Bell, treas.; John M. Adkins, sec.; W. L. D. Johnson, R. G. Lockett, L. H. Spivey, W. E. Miller, Andy Parr, N. Q. Henderson. The following compose the present board of directors: E. O. Smith, pres.; John Adkins, sec.; J. B. Bell, treas.; Sam Wilson, L. H. Spivey, R. G. Lockett, W. L. D. Johnson, Andy Parr and N. Q. Henderson. Librarian, Miss Bessie E. Osborne.

HOUSTON INDUSTRIAL COLLEGE

HOUSTON COLLEGE SETTLEMENT ASSOCIATION.

Four years ago this organization was effected through a call of the people around the college by President F. W. Gross. At first the people were a little suspicious, but decided to come and see. When the purpose was explained to the satisfaction of those present, no further trouble was experienced. At first the work was done by the teachers of the school in a very casual way, but two years ago the school was able to send out one of its teachers for a part of her time almost daily, and at once the work became well established and a definite part of the extension service of the college.

The following have been accomplished: A religious survey, a social and hygienic survey have been made; gardens have been planted; better housing and living are everywhere in evidence; noises both night and day have been abated; a better understanding about rearing children and the purpose of clean street, alleys, yards and houses have been clearly set forth.

Colored Schools of Houston

By PROF. E. O. SMITH

PROF. E. O. SMITH

In discussing a subject like this, one is bewildered by the mass of material—the thousand things which might properly enter into it. One might occupy almost the entire space allotted with facts and figures, table after table of statistics might be added, from each one of which many profitable deductions could be made. But in this article we shall attempt to tell as plainly and as simply as we can the story of what is being accomplished in the City of Houston by and for the colored people, resorting to statistics only when these are necessary for convincing evidence or for brevity, or both.

The educational problem in the entire South is a very complicated one and a very expensive one. In organization and effectiveness Houston has much that is worthy of emulation. The system of government in vogue was not originated in Houston, but the effective manner in which it has been worked out in all of its various departments almost entitles it to be known as the Houston Idea of Organization. This idea, in brief, is simply to select the best available man for a given line of work; hold him strictly responsible for its performance; give him authority to get it done in the most effective way. If he proves either unwilling or unable to do the work, put some one else in his place.

In the general government only the Mayor and four Commissioners are elected by the people. Upon these rests the whole responsibility of the city. These gentlemen divide the work among themselves. One man has charge of the finances of the city, another is in charge of the streets, another controls the police and fire departments, while still another looks after the water, light and health departments.

The Commissioners have power to appoint sub-officials who are responsible directly to themselves. For instance, the chief of police, the city attorney, the fire chief and others, each of whom employs the same general plan. The chief of police selects his officers, who are directly responsible to him. The same is true of other departments.

Pursuing this idea still further, the Commissioners appoint a School Board, which is clothed with absolute authority in school matters. The School Board accomplishes its work by means of several standing committees, as (1) Committee on Teachers; (2) Textbooks and Courses of Study; (3) Buildings, Furniture and Supplies; (4) Finance; (5) Rules, Grievances and Complaints. Each committee has authority to act and is held strictly accountable for its work. The Superintendent is elected by the Board and like other heads of departments, he has liberty, responsibility and authority. His sub-officers are the principals of the various schools and they are responsible to him for the management of the schools.

The colored schools, like the other schools, may be likened to the spokes of a wheel. Each is separate and apart but all are members of a great system. It is difficult to discuss them apart from the system because they are so closely interwoven with the schools in general. The same general course of study which is followed in the white schools obtains in the colored schools   The same supervisors who outline the work in the schools for white children outline it also for the colored schools, in fact, identical work is demanded in the white and colored schools   In the essentials—instruction, discipline and co-operation—there is no difference   In the matter of reports the same requirements exist for the white and colored schools   A close study of these will reveal the fact that the only difference between the white and colored schools in general is that the white schools have expanded certain phases of the work further and have added some courses leading to aesthetic development which the colored schools do not have, and secondly, that the equipment, including buildings, grounds, etc , and in fact the entire mechanical outfit employed in the white schools is much more expensive than in the colored schools   Aside from this the two are identical

SCHOLASTIC POPULATION

The population of Houston, according to the census of 1910, was 78,800, but according to the city directory of 1914 it was 129,570   Of this number the scholastic population was 24,064, of which 6,729 were colored and 17,335 were white   The net enrollment, white and colored, for the year of 1913-14 was 16,604, of which 11,518 were white and 5,086 were colored   To house these 5,086 colored children twelve different centers were made use of and designated Colored High School, Langston School, Luckie School, Douglass School, Gregory School, Booker T Washington School, Harper School, Bruce School, Dunbar School, Glen Cove School, Green Pond School and Bray's Bayou School

CAPACITY AND COST

These schools contain 112 rooms and 3,870 seats   The properties on which they are situated are valued at $53,000 and the buildings at $81,800   In addition to this the furniture and fixtures are valued at $15,825, making an entire valuation of $150,625

It is the custom in Houston to name the school buildings after illustrious and patriotic men of our country and so, among the white schools, we find such names as "Longfellow," "Crockett," "Sherman" and "Travis"   The colored schools likewise have selected names that honor the memory of distinguished sons of Ham   A little of this history of those whose names have been thus selected is surely not out of place

DOUGLASS SCHOOL

The Douglass School, which has an enrollment of 850, is our largest ward school   It was named after the great Frederick Douglass, a man who, though born in slavery, achieved fame as a statesman and an orator   He is said to have possessed the most melodious voice of any of the great orators which our country has produced   Every one knows how effectively he used it in arousing the country against slavery and in securing the assistance of such men as Henry Ward Beecher, William Lloyd Garrison and Abraham Lincoln

LANGSTON SCHOOL

The Langston School was named in honor of John M Langston who was the first colored man to graduate from Oberlin College and who spent a long, useful life, occupying many positions of honor and trust with the greatest satisfaction

BRUCE SCHOOL

The Bruce School derived its name from Blanch K Bruce of Mississippi, who for four or five times was appointed Register of the United States Treasury, and whose signature appears on more bills of various denominations, perhaps than any other man

DUNBAR SCHOOL

The Dunbar School was named for Paul Lawrence Dunbar, the greatest of colored poets Mr Wm Dean Howells said of him that he "introduced a new phase into American literature '

HARPER SCHOOL

The Harper School is the only one of the colored schools named for a woman It was so called in memory of Frances Harper, a writer of no small note, whose verses and songs have touched the hearts of thousands

BOOKER T WASHINGTON SCHOOL

The Booker T Washington School is peculiar in that it is the only school in the entire city which was named for a living man But so great is the admiration in which Booker T Washington, the wizard of Tuskegee, is held, that when his name was proposed to the School Board it was adopted without thought of its effect upon custom

LUCKIE SCHOOL

The Luckie School was named after Prof Chas Luckie, who was for many years a teacher at Prairie View College, sacrificing his very life for the young men and women of his race

With the exception of the High School and the Gregory School the other schools are mostly schools which have been taken in by the expansion of the city and have not yet been dedicated to the memory of illustrious heroes

To teach the 5,086 colored children, exactly one hundred colored teachers were employed A large majority of these were graduates of the Prairie View Normal and Industrial School, which is supported by the State There were, however, several from the best schools and universities open to colored people Among the schools outside the State, Fisk University at Nashville, Tenn , had the largest representation Other schools were Atlanta University, situated at Atlanta, Ga , Wilberforce University, in Ohio, Calabar College, in the West Indies, New Orleans University, Leland University, Tuskegee University, Wiley University, Bishop College, Mississippi State Normal, Paul Quinn College, Alcorn College Mary Allen Seminary, Portland High School, Staten (N Y) High School, Galveston High School and Houston High School An alphabetical list of all the teachers is attached hereto

SALARIES

The salaries paid colored teachers in Houston are on the whole not so high as are paid by other cities of the same class The schedule follows

Supernumerary—

First year, per month	$ 15 00
Second year, per month	20 00

Primary and Intermediate—

First year, per month	$ 40 00
Second year per month	45 00
Third year, per month	50 00
Fourth year, per month	55 00
Fifth year, per month	60 00
Sixth year, per month	65 00
Seventh year per month	70 00

Principals of Elementary Schools—

Two-room buildings	$ 70 00
Four-room buildings	80 00
Six-room buildings	90 00
Each room over six	2 00

High School—

Principals	$133 33
Vice-Principals	85 00
Assistants	80 00

NIGHT SCHOOL

The Houston plan of school government is decidedly democratic It believes that it is impossible to make good men and women of all of the boys and girls but it believes that it is the duty of the schools to give every person who desires to improve his condition an equal opportunity Because a man or boy is compelled to labor all day to make a living is no reason why the State should fail to provide an opportunity for his mental development, if any one is to be shown any special assistance it should be the man who after a hard day's digging in ditches or elsewhere is willing to spend an hour or two after night digging out the precious gems of knowledge The night schools for colored people were begun in 1911-12 and to give an idea of what was accomplished that first year, I shall quote from the Superintendent's annual report (page 25) "The Board last year established for the first time a night school for Negroes It was in the Bruce School in the Fifth Ward, with E O Smith as principal Over one hundred Negroes attended regularly, and the results were such as to fully justify the school Among those attending was one Negro 72 years old who worked all day in the cotton seed oil mill, and attended school three nights out of the week What do you suppose was his object in attending school? He said that he came because he wanted to learn to read the Bible In his early days he had not had the opportunity of learning to read and write, and, although he had been fond of the Bible he had known it only by hearing it read It is gratifying to be able to record that during one term of the night school he made such progress as to enable him, with more or less difficulty, to read the book of his choice and of his affection While he was the oldest person enrolled in our night schools, his case is simply typical of the work that our night schools are doing in dozens of instances" The number of night schools has now grown to four and the enrollment increased from one hundred to six hundred and sixty-four

Of course, the literary work is confined to the essentials reading, writing and arithmetic but it is considered quite as essential to know how to sew, to cook and do manual work as to improve one's self mentally so the Board has provided an opportunity to learn these things also The same teachers who have charge of these departments during the day conduct the classes at night It is gratifying to record that many cooks and house servants have embraced this opportunity as a means of rendering themselves more efficient in their daily tasks Many women who knew little or nothing of sewing have learned to do practically all of the plain sewing for their families and many of the men and boys who would otherwise have been awkward with tools have learned to make many useful pieces of mission furniture and saved much in the way of carpenter's bills by doing themselves much of the ordinary building needed around their homes

During the present year there has been a new feature introduced into the colored schools A class was trained in Civil Service work As is well known, many young colored men find employment in this field To enable them to compete successfully the most efficient drill possible was given them by one experienced in such matters Thus Houston is doing whatever seems wisest and best in encouraging those who are anxious to make themselves better citizens

LIBRARY

Another very important adjunct to the public schools is the public library It not only aids the schools in doing this work efficiently, but it takes up the work where they leave off and continues it on through life For many years it has been the policy of the Houston schools to have an annual library day No compulsion is used Envelopes are given each child in school with the request that he return it with or without a contribution In this way no child is humiliated since no child knows whether the envelope contains money or not By this means a number of books have been bought in sets of 40 each, which are kept at the public library and loaned to the various schools to be used as supplementary work Houston is the only city in the South that has a Carnegie library for colored people and they are rightly proud of it It is situated near the High School in the very heart of the densest settlement of colored people

INSTITUTES

Not the least of the features of the schools of Houston is the monthly institute The work done is strictly professional Educational principles are studied and discussed The time is divided into two periods of one hour ecah During one hour some educator of note is employed to deliver a lecture and during the other the time is given over to the study of a text book Among those who have lectured before the institute have been Dr Bliss Perry of Harvard, Dr A Caswell Ellis of the University of Texas, Dr Booker T Washington of Tuskegee. E L Blackshear of Prairie View, Dr W S Sutton of the University of Texas, Dr G A Shands of Southwestern University, Dr A E Winship of Boston, Dr Edward Vance Cook, Dr Henry S Curtis Mr J A Puffer and other men of international reputation To spend a term of years as a teacher in Houston is equivalent to spending the time in the average normal school as will be evident upon considering the list of books which teachers have been required to use in their institutes Among them are Painter's History of Education, James' Psychology, Spencer's Education, Everyday Problems in Teaching, by Horn, How to Study and How to Teach Children to Study, by McMurray, School Room Essentials, by P W Horn, All the Children of All the People, by Dr O Shea, The Boy Problem, by Forbush, The Recitation, by McMurray, The Principles of Education, by Thorndyke, The Best Things in Our Schools, by Horn and like works In addition to this there is held each month a grade meeting where all the teachers having the same grades assemble and under the leadership of a person of ' experience, discuss the best methods of putting into practice the educational principles which are discussed in the institutes Thus it is seen that two hours each month are devoted to the study of educational principles and one hour to the use of devices Young teachers find these meetings invaluable and all teachers find them interesting and instructive

MOTHERS CLUBS

Still another feature of which the Houston schools are proud is the system of Mothers Clubs which are connected with the various schools The duties of the Mothers' Clubs may be summarized as five First It must be busied with some definite, specific undertaking Second It must work in co-operation with the regular school authorities Third Its work should be partly utilitarian and partly cultural In other words, the mothers should attempt to accomplish something definite for the good of the schools and also something of a cultural nature for themselves   Fourth   The work for the schools should supplement the work of the Board   It should be along some line that the School Board is not likely to undertake, or else should go a little further than the Board is likely to go   A Mothers' Club should not undertake to do what the School Board could, should and probably would do   Fifth   Its work should be an undertaking not so large as to be beyond the reasonable expectation that the organization will be likely to carry it through   Work of this kind among the colored people is new and difficult   The altruistic spirit has not as yet asserted itself to any marked extent and yet the Superintendent asserts that he considers them the most valuable of all the agencies which are lending a helping hand to our schools

Since their organization six years ago they have raised and expended for the benefit of the colored schools the sum of $3,989 15   This money was spent in various ways   Much of it was spent in furnishing the different schools with pianos so that the children might march in and out of the buildings to the sound of good music   At one building the mothers employed a sewing teacher   At another they bought a machine and sewing tables   Elsewhere they furnished swings and outdoor gymnasia, phonographs and slides have been supplied, a cistern built and sanitary lunches furnished the children at nominal cost   Book cases have been procured where they have been needed   In some sections it has been customary to grade the yards and in others attention has been given to the beautification of the school grounds   So that to the extent that the clubs have co-operated with the school authorities, supplementing and expanding the work being done to that extent they are a success   It is true that, like the tides, "they ebb and flow," but, also, "like the brook, they go on forever," doing the little things which are necessary but which would often be impossible except for such an agency

FOUR STORIES

There is in our country today a wide difference of opinion in regard to the education of the Negro   There are advocates of this kind of training and defenders of another kind and those who believe in all kinds and those who believe in none at all   Many of these people are absolutely conscientious   Their opinion is simply an opinion, however, and proves nothing one way or another   After all there is but one way to judge such things without malice and that is to appreciate or reject these in accordance with their fruit   "By their fruits ye shall know them "

Four little stories told by the Superintendent illustrate in a very vital way what the colored schools are doing for their people and for the community in general

FIRST STORY

Readers of our local papers are familiar with the name of Nicodemus—or used to be   He was not exactly a headliner but his name was formerly good for a few inches of space in the police columns almost any day   By the time he was twelve years old he was a professional jail bird   He was a petty thief, housebreaker and general juvenile offender   Incidently he did not know A from B, he was too young to send to the penitentiary and too bad to leave out of it   Our juvenile court law had gone just far enough to make it impossible to do anything with him   He had been arrested repeatedly jailed and turned loose again   The officers were hopefully awaiting the time when he would be old enough to send to the penitentiary

While matters were in this condition it came about one day that the teachers of Booker T Washington School, of which E O Smith is principal, became interested in Nicodemus   They asked him why he did not go to school   He told them that he had once tried to enter one of our colored schools and had been refused admittance on account of his general record as an undesirable They told him that the Booker T Washington School would be glad to take him—and to keep him so long as he behaved himself Nicodemus decided that the experiment might be worth trying, at any rate he did not see how it could make matters much worse with him The result was that he secured a primer and entered the low first grade along with the little tots who were just starting They knew as much as he did—about books at any rate He not only started but he stuck It caused a mild sensation among colored circles when it was learned that Nicodemus had been in school a month and had not burned the school house down or stolen it The man for whom he did odd jobs in return for which he was given a place to sleep, was one of the first to notice the change and to comment upon it The Superintendent heard of it and began to take a little friendly interest in Nicodemus He sent word that when the boy could read every lesson in the book he would give him another That book was soon called for and was delivered with the word that when this was finished there would be another one sent Soon after the Superintendent heard him read the last lesson in this book and gave him another with the inscription "To Nicodemus as a Reward for Good Conduct " This inscription seemed to please Nicodemus, though the idea was rather a novel one to him It was, probably the first time he had been told that his conduct was good He spoke of these books as "The ones the boss man gave me " When Nicodemus was forced, on account of sickness, to be absent a day from school he anxiously sent word as to the cause lest his teacher might think he had gone back to his old ways In one year's time he had transformed from an incorrigible thief and jail bird to an industrious, hard working Negro boy One excellent feature is that he is not proud of his past record He has even dug up another name which he says is his right name He refuses to be known any longer as Nicodemus I do not give his new name, because it is not right that he should be embarrassed by his past I predict that he will make a useful, intelligent, industrious man of his race He may make another Booker T Washington or E L Blackshear If our colored schools can work such changes with boys like Nicodemus, they are worth all we are paying for them—and more

STORY TWO

This is the story of Lettie Smith I do not know that I can tell it better than by quoting the exact words of a personal letter which I received last winter from a Houston lady of culture and refinement 'I think that as Superintendent of the Houston schools you would perhaps be interested if I were to tell you some of the things I have noticed about Lettie Smith, the little colored girl who now works for me as nurse and house girl She is a pupil of the high third grade at Hollywood School (of which Mabel Wesley is principal)

"My attention was first called to her work by the respectful manner in which she spoke of her teacher and her childish longing for school Next I found her recognizing the portraits of Longfellow, Whittier and other American poets, which she saw on the walls of our library She would tell little stories of their childhood, which she said that she had read at school She noticed some raffia mats that I have, and readily told how and of what they were made She often sings little patriotic songs to the baby and tries to teach her rhymes and memory gems She usually gets good grades on her report card and she says that she can't bear to hear children mouth over their reading

'She has evidently had a good, earnest, sensible teacher It is remarkable to me that the public schools are doing so well for the colored children—and for the white children, too, for that matter I think that Lettie compares at least fairly well in advancement with the average white child of her age and grade "

The Superintendent remarks that "the fact that an educated Houston woman, a house keeper and the wife of one of Houston's good citizens, thought it worth while to write the Superintendent this letter, speaks well not only for her own kind-heartedness and appreciation, but also for the work our colored schools are doing.'

STORY THREE

This is a very short story. One day a Houston lady met the Superintendent on the street and said to him: "I want to speak a good word for your Langston Colored School. I have a cook who has been trained in the Domestic Science department of that school and she is the neatest, most cleanly, most economical cook I have ever had, and also one of the best cooks. If the Langston can train up some more like her, it will be doing a wonderful service not only for the Negroes, but also for the white people of the city."

STORY FOUR

This also will be told in briefest outline. It is about one of our colored teachers who told me that she expected to raise one hundred dollars to help establish some form of industrial work at her building. The climax of the story is, that after continued effort she raised it. She did so by a number of concerts, musical entertainments, etc., gotten up chiefly with the help of the children, given for an admittance fee of ten cents. It takes quite a time to raise a hundred dollars in ten cent sums, but this Negro woman accomplished it. It must have been a case of heaven helps those who help themselves. She remarked to me last year that if the School Board would next year give her enough equipments to teach laundry work, she would be glad to teach it. I most heartily recommend that the equipment be provided.

I have related these stories just as the Superintendent told them, and I believe they illustrate more vividly than could be shown otherwise the industry, sacrifice and devotion which the Negro teacher is giving to the schools. We could continue stories indefinitely of this kind. We could tell how the teacher of Latin out of her hard-earned savings spent a year in Rome that she might be better prepared to do her work. Several of the teachers do research work during the summer vacation. The colored schools are doing a wonderful work for the community. Some years ago when a large area of the city was destroyed by fire, a colored school was opened for the use of the sufferers and colored teachers employed themselves in securing food and clothing for the needy.

From the foregoing we see clearly that all the bodies mentioned are parts of the community. It is for the community that the schools exist and the more ways they find of serving the community the greater is their value. The colored schools are serving the community in many ways, but as the Superintendent says, if they did naught but reclaim and develop such characters as Nicodemus "they would justify all of the money that is spent upon them—and more."

Progress of Negro Churches In Houston Since Emancipation or the Civil War

By Rev. W. H. Logan, District Superintendent of the Houston District,
Texas Conference, Methodist Episcopal Church.

One of the speakers of "The Flying Squadron" who visited Houston during a temperance rally in this city some time since, said among other things: "Five things go to make up civilization. They are the home, the church, the school, the printing press and political life."

Properly understood and appreciated by the masses, the church should by the very nature of things permeate the school, sanctify the printing press and purify political life. The home and the church are very close of kin, having been associated in the mission of race uplift since the days of faithful Abraham.

The Negro race is characteristically religious, the religious element standing out in bold relief not only with the native bush man in Africa, but the slaves in their abject ignorance on their master's plantation showed it in a marked degree.

Some good intentioned people believe that the Negroes on the plantations observed certain forms of worship because it was one of the exactions of masters and overseers; but that belief is not well founded, for there were many masters and overseers who tried to suppress the religious emotions of their slaves, but all to no purpose, for the Negroes on such plantations almost invariably disregarded such efforts at suppressing their pent-up spiritual feelings and would steal away by night and present their petitions to the unseen Spirit and would do so at the peril of their lives in some instances.

The Negroes in the City of Houston have made wonderful progress in religious development, if the number of members, in church and Sunday School, church property owned and church sittings are to be reckoned as factors in arriving at a fair estimate of the standing of the several denominations that have representation here.

The Baptist and Methodist were the only denominations that had members among the Negroes in Houston at the close of the Civil war. Of those two denominations there were only two societies, they merging from connection with the white members of those two persuasions into independent churches of free men, being today the two leading churches among Negroes in Houston, and are known far and wide as the Antioch Baptist Church and the Trinity Methodist Episcopal Church. The Trinity Church site is the most valuable piece of real estate owned by any denomination or society in the State, if not in the entire South, among Negroes.

From this small beginning of Negro churches fifty years ago, there are more than twenty Negro Baptist churches in the city with fully ten thousand members. There are about three thousand five hundred Methodists, with sixteen meeting houses in the city, including three branches of the Methodist family. The Baptists and Methodists had for their leaders and pastors in the beginning of freedom in 1865 two powerful men in the persons of Revs. Sandy Parker and Elias Dibble.

These two remarkable characters, having had training by their white pastors as expounders of the Word of God in the trying days of slavery, used that training to good account, serving as mediums between the hot heads of both races, teaching their people to seek the friendship and good will of their white neighbors.

The Methodists, led by their war-time pastor, Elias Dibble, being allowed to remove their little chapel from the site of the First Methodist Episcopal Church, South, which they had erected in ante-bellum days in the rear of the white church on Texas Avenue between Travis and Milam Streets bought a whole block of ground, retaining half of it for church purposes and sold the other half to members of the church The fact that Bro Dibble sought to settle members around the church within their own homesteads shows he was a man of vision and the further fact that he retained one-half of the block for church purposes he read the future correctly, the act looked at from any angle, shows that he saw future greatness for Houston Methodism From that small beginning with Trinity as the only Methodist Church in the city, nine other chapels and churches are now in existence Trinity being the mother, making ten in all Trinity is not only the mother of the other Methodist Episcopal churches in the city, but she is the fore runner of the sister Methodist churches, the African Methodist Episcopal Church and the Colored Methodist Episcopal Church, the former numbering 1,500 members with seven church houses and the latter with one meeting house and two or three hundred members It was easier for these latter churches to build in Houston by reason of the pioneer work done by Trinity in giving emphasis to Methodist doctrine, creating a deep sentiment in the community, conducive to the growth of Methodism irrespective of the divisions in the family name Father Dibble and those associated with him in working out the problems immediately concerning the religious and moral elevation of the free Negroes in Houston did not stop at securing a church home, but they took the lead in the purchase of the Emancipation Park, the Olive Wood Cemetery and the organization of a Mutual Benevolent Society The ministry in those days was not a one-sided ministry, but an all-round ministry, serving the people in every way possible, looking toward the formation of a better citizenship

Rev Sandy Parker led his people from what used to be called Baptist Hill on Rusk Street to the present site of Antioch Church on Robin Street between Frederick and Shaw, and was succeeded by the late Rev J Yates, who guided the church with a masterful hand, erecting possibly the first brick meeting house owned by the Negro race in the State of Texas

In the early nineties that church edifice was remodeled the architect and builder being Robt Jones, who is still living In 1909 that church underwent a complete renovation, being greatly enlarged and beautified, in its present form being one of the most substantial and commodious church edifices in the entire South owned by Negroes

That work was done under the pastorate of Dr F L Lights, the present pastor, who entered upon the 22nd year's service during the month of March, 1915 That church occupies a unique place in race history, in that it has had but three pastors in 50 years

Father Yates established Houston College with the assistance of two noble Home Missionary workers in the persons of Misses Peck and Dysart, which institution is accomplishing a great work under that firm and resolute educator, Prof F W Gross, A M

The African Methodist Episcopal Church is fast forging to the front, having begun its work in this city in the early seventies, its interests have been looked after by an efficient band of faithful pastors Wesley Chapel its principal church, is an aggressive organization

The Colored Methodist Episcopal Church was later still in coming into the city, but since its coming in the middle eighties it has one very good church and a healthy mission and is destined to play an important part in the racial uplift and religious welfare of the citizens of Houston

About ten years ago the Congregational Church established a church here among our people and that denomination has a neat little church edifice, a growing membership, an efficient pastor and is an indispensable factor in the religious and race life of our city

The Church of God, another organization of recent origin about which the writer knows little, has a place no doubt, and will work in unison with the other churches of the city "And John answered and said, Master, we saw one casting out devils in Thy name, and we forbade him, because he followeth not with us And Jesus said unto him, Forbid him not for he that is not against us is for us '

As we look back over the past many notable achievements have been accomplished by the churches, in the erection of larger and better church houses, the increase of members in church and Sunday School being true as it relates to the masses of the people, to say nothing of the reformation in many individual lives But the work of the church organization for the years that lie immediately before us will require not only an efficient ministry, but a much more active, aggressive and liberal membership

The day for the unworthy preacher will not come as long as laymen are tolerant of men as pastors whom they know to be unworthy of support Instead of the frequent rally, including the begging lists put into the hands of women and girls to run down the men of the community to get money to run the church of tomorrow, the members of the various churches will have to learn the beauty of giving out of their earnings to support churches and preachers

No beggar of any age, not an invalid, has ever commanded the respect of industrious people nor will the Negro Church of tomorrow command the respect of honest people until it proves beyond a shadow of doubt that encumstances force it to call on the public after exhausting every reasonable effort to discharge its own financial obligations

The church of tomorrow will be expected to stimulate a wholesome, moral sentiment not by placing the bars so high that the reprobate and the sinner need not apply for membership, but by maintaining such high moral grounds within the membership that the spiritual atmosphere may be like a running stream of water, purifying itself as it flows and cleansing those who may by faith seek healing in its waters "And everything shall live whither the river cometh "

The business of the church is to save men It does not just exist to give the pastor a living, but that through the instrumentality of the pastor and the members, the unregenerate may find salvation the sin-sick healing to their souls

Efficiency is the watchword in every calling and avocation of life, more especially in the Church of Jesus Christ Not only is there great need for efficient pastors, but for stewards and deacons trustees and members It is no encouragement to an efficient, clean minister to devote himself to such preparation through the week and by the aid of the Holy Spirit the proper use of books, the study of men as he comes in contact with them to give time and energy for necessary preparation to be told after the sermon, that he gave a fine lecture To properly appreciate the efforts of the consecrated minister, the pew must keep abreast of the times

How many of our laymen read religious books or newspapers? I make bold the assertion that many of our laymen who subscribe for the denominational papers never unwrap them, much less read them It requires an effort to adopt the habit of reading good books and papers Oh! For a prepared ministry and a prepared laity!

One would have to be exceedingly dull not to rejoice at the victories won by the churches of Houston for the past fifty years, but if the fathers accomplished so much in their day without school advantages without the higher ideals of life in the home, what ought their sons and successors accomplish with these helps?

The church of tomorrow will have to erect its edifices so as to furnish departments for every phase of innocent amusement, social centers etc, so as to hold the young people and train them in works of mercy and help "Offer unto God thanksgiving and pay thy vows unto the Most High The church of tomorrow, if she avails herself of the opportunity which lies within her grasp, may inscribe upon her banner this motto 'Out of Zion, the perfection of beauty God hath shined "

Brief Sketch of Houston Baptists

BY F. L. LIGHTS, D. D.

I am called upon to give the history of the Baptists of the City of Houston. History is an account of that which is known to have occurred, a record of the past and a narrative of events.

This historical sketch is a narrative of the development and growth of the Baptists of the City of Houston from its beginning to the present.

Just after the war a great religious wave of rejoicing and the shout of Hallelujah went up from the hearts of thousands of our people. They assembled, but not in an organized form, merely in mass meeting, and preached and prayed and sang until January 1st, 1866; that is to say from the 19th of June, 1865, until January 1st, 1866, they were preparing to organize the first colored Baptist Church, which was organized by Rev. Crane, white minister, in the white Baptist Church with twelve members and on the same day seven others were united by baptism.

They worshiped in a white Baptist church a few weeks and then worshiped in the German Baptist Church on McKinney Street a short while. The Germans desired to repair the house, therefore they were compelled to find other quarters. However, during the time they worshiped in the white church Rev. J. B. Lynk (white) was the pastor. About this time Rev. I. S. Campbell, the first missionary appointed by the Home Missionary Society for the colored people of Texas, made his appearance in the city. The Baptists were again out of doors and like sheep without a shepherd. He preached his first sermon on the first Sunday in August, 1866. I. S. Campbell and J. J. Rhyenhart organized the Antioch Baptist Church.

Thence followed the Mt. Zion Baptist Church in the Second Ward, known as Frost Town, and other Baptist churches began to spring up. The Lincoln Baptist Association was organized in the Antioch Baptist Church in 1867. God's divine presence rested on the churches, led by Brothers Sandy Parker, Rev. J. Yates, Rev. H. Stewart, Dr. H. Watts, G. W. Booker and the host of other ministers. Soon there were churches in all sections of the city. A great awakening followed in 1870, 1871 and 1872. Hundreds believed and were baptized, magnificent houses of worship were built by the churches and property began to increase in value, and in 1880 the Woman's Missionary Society sent Misses Peck and Dysart, who began the teaching of the women and children in the way of the Lord, and the work grew and prospered, and some excellent missionary workers were developed. They, through the Missionary Society, gave us Houston College, a well-equipped school for the training of our boys and girls and ministerial students. The school began in the fall of 1885 by Rev. J. Yates, J. W. Watson, S. B. Sumerville, D. M. Williams, Misses F. Dysart and J. L. Peck. Until October, 1894, it was operated in a small rented building in the city. September 1, 1894, the foundation of two splendid buildings were laid by the untiring efforts of Misses Dysart, J. L. Peck and the other trustees, Yates and Watson. The first principals were Misses Dysart and Peck. It has had the following presidents since its organization: Dr. J. H. Garnet, A. R. Griggs, D. D., D. A. Scott, D. D., F. W. Bloodsaw and Prof. F. W. Gross.

The fall session was opened in one of the new buildings, that today is prepared to teach the students along business lines, such as carpentry, bricklaying, laundry work, nursing, sewing and all domestic science and manual training. From this small beginning we have developed to the number of 54 organized Baptist churches in the City of Houston.

with a membership of about ten thousand, beautiful, well-appointed houses of worship, property located in some of the best localities of the city. The ministry of the city is abreast with the time. Progressive, intelligent and moral leaders worthy of the name.

The Baptists have the largest membership, numerically, in the city. They are growing in intellect and finance. Some of the wealthiest citizens are members of the Baptist churches, a large number of men and women of the professional teachers, lawyers, doctors, professors, real estators and in every profession and walk of life are members of the regular Missionary Baptist Church. May it be said to the credit of our great denomination that we are helping to shape the members of our race for their future destiny and to play their part in the drama of life and to work for peace, concord and unity among all the races and the lifting up of Jesus Christ, Who is the standard of perfection.

From year to year many of the graduates from our High School are members of the Baptist Churches and these go from the High School to the colleges and seminaries to finish their education. We have such talented ministers as Drs W M Johnson, N T Lane H B Southern, E H Branch, W M Sauls, C W Holmes, H R Johnson, D H Rankins, R L Williams, P R McGriff, A A Gordon, A S Gordon, G R Altred, J W Edwards C H Hunt, D Hawkins, D H Griffin, C H Smith, N P Pullum and a host of others too numerous to mention, all pastoring self-supporting churches. The Baptists of Houston have had a great harvest of souls during the year 1915. The greatest revival ever held in Houston was in 1907 when 743 souls were converted in Antioch Baptist Church pastored by the Rev F L Lights, D D. These converts were united with the various churches of the city. Antioch received into her membership by baptism that year more than 100. We praise God for Houston College, one of the best equipped schools according to its size in the State. Its sanitary conditions are excellent, its discipline and management cannot be surpassed. All honor to Professor F W Gross and the faculty of Houston College.

We hail with joy the environment of a Christian institution. We also have the Western Star Publishing Company, our Baptist paper, managed by Prof E D Pierson, teacher of the Senior Grammar department in the High School, a Bachelor of Sciences from Bishop College, Drs L K Williams of Ft Worth, and A R Griggs, of Dallas, editors, Dr F L Lights president of the company.

The paper is a great moulder of sentiment for the moral uplift of all the people.

The Baptists own almost a million dollars worth of property in Houston.

God has done great things for us and will do great things with us in morality chastity, virtue temperance and intellectual development of all the people and keeping peace, harmony and tranquillity among the races. May the good work march on down through the centuries, redeeming the times because the days are evil.

♣ INDUSTRIAL LIFE IN THE UNITED STATES ♣

In order to get some idea of the industrial and professional advancement made by members of the Afro-American race in the United States, it is only necessary to go back one-half a century and compare the conditions then and those now

Of all races that have come up out of slavery, it can be said without flattery that the Afro-American race has shown the greatest advancement along industrial, religious, educational and professional lines of any race that has only been emancipated a single half century.

When the Civil war liberated the four millions of people held as slaves in the Southern States, they possessed very little of this world's goods and had made small advancement in the lines noted above

So that the results shown by the United States census of 1910 are the results gained in fifty short years, less than two full generations of people

While the reading of figures and tables ordinarily is of little interest and very boring in its nature, still the reading of the dry figures which represent the advancements made under hard conditions, of a people who have only been out of bondage for such a short time, which reveal beneath and between them many stories of hard struggle and determination and many, many battles fought and won under handicap, must be of interest to the race which has accomplished this and should be of interest to all peoples in any way connected with them

The cross of their capture and sale into slavery has been turned into the crown of their endeavor as seen today, in their homes, their schools, their churches, their establishments and their better conditions of life and livelihood

This advancement is shown best by summarizing those owning and those engaged in various industrial and professional groups

The professional class is represented by a total of nearly 130,000, or, to be exact as to the figures given in the 1910 census 128,303 This is, of course somewhat less than the figures now, and they more nearly approach the first figure given

Of the professional class of Afro-Americans in the United States the latest available figures give the following

Those in public service, that is, government service, 69,471, clergymen, 17,495, judges and justices, 19, attorneys, 779, authors 27, editors, 146, journalists, 25, dentists, 478, physicians and surgeons, male, 2,744, female, 333, trained nurses, male, 275, female, 2 158, musicians, male, 2,769, female 605, music teachers, male 490, female 1,742, school teachers, male, 6,219, female, 22 528

Those engaged in mines and mining represent a group of 62 496 laborers and 79 operators divided as follows

	Workers	Owners		Workers	Owners
Coal mining	40,603	12	Lead, zinc, etc	5,066	13
Gold and platinum	303	2	Quarries	10,348	28
Iron mining	5,376	14	Oil wells	266	6
Copper mining	282	2	Salt wells	234	4

The manufacturing interest is represented by a long list of industries and shows the largest group of operators and laborers In the list is also included the contractors and builders This list totals to 974,918 If to this you add the 1 300 000 who are engaged in domestic and laundry service, etc , and the nearly three million that are engaged in agricultural pursuits, and the number not classified, you have a total of nearly six millions of Afro-Americans engaged in gainful pursuits

This is about eighty per cent of those of the race who are in the working age that is, between 10 and 65 years of age As compared with the white race this is about twice as many per thousand engaged in gainful pursuits

To give you an idea of the varied industries and the number engaged in them, as given by the 1910 census, the following list is given You will note that this does not include the barbers, retail porters, nor cleaners and pressers etc, in the United States who are making their own way This is indeed a remarkable industrial showing in a race that, including babies, children, aged, infirm and all, does not yet reach the ten million mark, according to the 1910 census report

	Workers	Owners		Workers	Owners
Fertilizer factories	7,723	6	Shoe factories	2,950	5
Paint factories	246	2	Tanners	2,272	10
Powder factories	125	4	Box factories	1,601	6
Soap factories	196	4	Furniture factories	4,254	48
Other chem factories	2,584	37	Pianos and organs	262	3
Brick and tile works	18,817	32	Saw and planing mills	111,223	219
Contractors and build-			Other wood works	8,668	44
ing trades, male	242,387	2,852	Clock and watch makers	52	8
Female	45,754	20	Goldsmiths	191	4
Glass factories	2,454	1	Tin and enamelware	1,299	23
Lime, cement, etc	4,486	22	Other metals	119	1
Marble and stone	1,788	15	Paper mills	1,273	1
Pottery	477	1	Publishing estab	5,048	173
Clothing factories	10,264	317	Carpet mills	279	9
Hats and gloves	234	1	Cotton mills	7,126	1
Shirts, collars, cuffs	1,094		Textile mills	645	62
Bakeries	3,448		Broom factories	784	30
Males		15	Charcoal and coke	5,454	19
Females		28	Cigars and tobacco	25,463	50
Butter and cheese	176	2	Turpentine distilleries	7,162	24
Candy	791	9	Miscellaneous	37,000	205
Flour and grist mills	2,251	29	Engaged in water trans-		
Slaughter and packing			portation	32,500	33
houses	5,178	4	Livery stables	21,000	323
Sugar factories	340	1	Street Railways	130,000	
Other food factories	4,594	23	Officials		1,015
Agricultural Implement			Postmasters	104	
factories	596	2	Postmistresses	49	
Auto factories	569	2	Postal clerks	702	
Blast furnace and steel			Banks and banking	3,208	
roller mills	18,222		Owners		9
Owners		5	Cashiers		67
Foremen		132	Insurance business	2,604	
Manufacturers car and			Head officials		100
R R works	4,425	1	Wholesale and retail		
Iron foundries	6,172	5	trade	122,000	
Ship and boat building	4,347	7	Wholesalers	241	

	Workers	Owners		Workers	Owners
Wagon and carriage building	2,000	9	Warehouses and cold storage	2 437	13
Other iron and steel works	5,427	32	Grain and elevator	670	5
Harness and leather	421	28	Public service not otherwise classified	26 250	
Leather cases and belts	97	4			

I will not stop to call your attention to the many startling and significant features of this report, except merely to ask you to read the list carefully and note the facts regarding ownership of different industries, factories and businesses which, no doubt, will surprise you

This list represents the life work and the very life blood of the best of the race It is an epitome of the good and the industriousness of this race so newly introduced to freedom in a land of the free What has been done in the past can be repeated with greater success in the future The Afro-American race is gradually but surely carving out its industrial and economic independence and doing it with the assistance and good will of the white race

WADE HAMPTON LOGAN

Wade Hampton Logan, son of Felix and Ann Maborne Logan is the fourth child of a family of eleven children nine boys and two girls

He was born in Paris, Lamar County, Texas, October 20th, 1857. Having first seen the light upon the farm, his first service to the world was pitched in that wholesome, helpful, care-free life of a farmer boy

His was a happy, self-possessed spirit, and whatever he was called upon to do, he entered upon that duty with the determination to do it as well if not better, than any one else, and this has been the winning characteristic of his most remarkable career

As the days of his early boyhood were spent in looking after the sheep, cattle and horses, he had a chance to study nature in its simplicity, and in studying nature he got a view of the sublime splendor and beauty of nature's God, which vision led up to his conversion August 16th, 1880, at the age of 23 years, under the preaching of Rev. Taylor Moore He was baptized by the late Rev. Daniel Battle and joined Mt. Zion Methodist Episcopal Church, Paris, Texas where he served faithfully as class leader, exhorter and local preacher until called to larger service

He is in the strictest sense a self-made man. Long days and nights, as his lean, gaunt form cast its shadow, young Logan could be seen with the old familiar Blue Back Speller in his hands digging out his alphabet

Being passionately fond of books he devoured every particle of reading matter that he was able to muster. And although it was at a time when such a thing as a Negro teacher was one of the curiosities yet the indomitable spirit and determination of this seeker after truth, enabled him to overcome all obstacles and take hold of his own boot straps and lift himself up and above his environments

So anxious was he to know the purposes of God in his own life, and so determined was he to have complete satisfaction as to the work of grace in his own soul, he rode 20 miles to borrow his brother Harrison's Bible and read it through before uniting with the church

The early struggles of successful men are familiar chapters in the world's history. By some instinct they seek the field in which their abilities will find the sphere of action to which they are best adapted

In 1881, in answer to the call of God, he came forward and was duly received into the Texas Conference and at the end of his second year, so very promising was his career, he was appointed to the pastorate of Trinity Church Houston, where he served the full term of three years

His persistent efforts and unflagging determination to better fit himself for his great life work made him a perpetual student and wherever he was appointed one of the first things that he did was to matriculate under some one who was able to teach him and continue his studies

Hence, at the expiration of eight years after joining the Conference he found himself prepared to assume the responsibility of a Presiding Elder, to which exalted position the church at this time saw fit to call him. He has been so honored three times, having served the Navasota and the Marshall districts. He is now serving his fourth year as District Superintendent of the Houston District. In 1895 he received the degree of Doctor of Divinity from Phylander Smith College, of Little Rock, Ark

He has arisen as a mighty force in Texas Methodism and stands high in the councils of the church   He has been elected to every General Conference on the first ballot for five consecutive quadrenniums, and served for eight years as a member of the Book Committee

His second call to Trinity came in 1900, and for more than nine years he fed the flock of God and led them on to conquest and victory

At a cost of $16,000 he erected the present Trinity building with its capacious auditorium and splendid appointments and retired with the delightful satisfaction of having paid every dollar

He was called from Trinity to Wesley Church, New Orleans, to meet and combat a legal situation there, and after two years of earnest effort he saved to that historic church two lots, a hall, and a splendid eight-room parsonage and then returned to his beloved Texas Conference, where his brethren have always delighted to honor him

As a District Superintendent he has but few equals in the church, and in the Texas Conference he has an unparalleled record   He has led in numerous church enterprises for Methodism, but soul-winning is his chief passion

He is a poor man, although he has held some of the best appointments in the church He is a poor man from choice, for he has never refused an appeal for help or turned a deaf ear to the voice of trouble

The vilest man who walks the streets can halt his hurried steps and get the price of a meal if hungry   He is brother to the men who serve with him   The troubles of any man on his district are the troubles of W H Logan

"Find out how much you owe and I will see what I can do for you," are words which have greeted the ears of many a struggling preacher on his district

For these years he has been constantly taking upon himself the burdens of other men and only for the love of making them happy   He is profoundly religious, but free from bigotry   He is indeed very human, but he is also very true and genuine

His business is as sacred as his religion

REV. WADE H. LOGAN, D. D.
District Superintendent Houston District M. E. Church

Trinity M. E. Church, 1410 Travis Street.

Rev. A. W. Carr   Alveria Carr   Mrs. A. W. Carr

ADOLPHUS WADE CARR

Adolphus Wade Carr was born in Orange, Orange County, Texas, June 10th, 1869. His father died when young Wade was but two years old, leaving five children to be cared for by a widowed mother. His mother moved to Galveston when he was four years of age and being a devout Christian and a loyal Methodist, she naturally found a church home for herself and children, placing them in Wesley Tabernacle Sunday School, Wade being among the first scholars of that now famous church. His early training was limited, as the school in those days was far behind the splendid system of today, but young Carr made the best of the opportunity and laid the foundation for the expansion of what has proven in later years to be a very bright mind. He loved books and has been a hard student all his life. Other children would be racing and playing—he would be in some secluded spot poring over Pilgrim's Progress by John Bunyan, or absorbed in the Bible. Early in life he did a most pleasing thing from his saintly mother's viewpoint, being converted at 18 years of age and united with the church of his mother's choice, Wesley Tabernacle, during the pastorate of Rev. V. M Cole. Being without a father's care and feeling deeply an affectionate son's love for a hard worked mother, at the tender age of 16 years he launched out in business for himself, doing whatever work he could find to make an honest living. He rose steadily in the estimation of all, going higher at each change, filling at one time a responsible position in the employ of the National Government during the incumbency of the late Norris Wright Cuney as Collector of Customs at the port of Galveston. In 1889 he was married to Miss Rachel Ann Willis, of Willis, Texas, to which union one sweet girl has been born, the pride of her father and mother. He felt called to the work of the Christian ministry early in life, but did not enter its arduous tasks until 1899, and then as a supply on what was called Red Oak Circuit, in the Marshall District, Presiding Elder W. H. Logan appointing him to that work that young Carr might have the chance to pursue his studies in Wiley University. He received a salary of $125 his first year, the support being so meager that he and his wife chopped cotton for 50 cents a day and picked cotton in the fall for 50 cents per hundred

He not only put full time in school the years he attended Wiley but did general reading of the best books he could secure and in that way built up a splendid vocabulary, which enables him now to prepare and preach some great sermons   He has one of the choicest libraries possessed by any preacher in our Conference

He joined the Texas Annual Conference in December, 1900, held in Marshall, under the presidency of Bishop I W Joyce and ever since his progress has been one steady march forward   While pastor of Lee Tabernacle, Navasota, he saw no possible way to relieve his church of its heavy debt without aid from outside sources   After consultation with certain interested members of the Conference in 1907, Bishop William Burt presiding, he introduced and the Conference adopted a resolution asking the Board of Home Missions and Church Extension to donate $1,500 towards liquidating the $3 000   The Board undertook the task, meeting the local church half way   Rev Carr raised the greater part of the amount of the debt the last two years of his pastorate, making possible the payment of the entire indebtedness by his successor the second year of his successor's incumbency   He built a fine parsonage during his first year at Paris and had launched a movement for a great church in Marshall, but before his plans matured for the carrying out of this plan an emergency arose in the Conference during 1913 which made his appointment to Trinity Church, Houston, imperative, where he is at this writing serving very acceptably his second year

He is noted for his use of printer's ink in connection with his pastoral work and for his sympathetic disposition towards the sick and suffering, not confining by any means his ministry of love to the members of his own church or of his denomination   Being in the very prime of life and with a laudable ambition his friends will be sadly disappointed if he is not heard from in the years that lie before him   He is Secretary of the Conference and it is a safe prophecy that greater honors and preferment await him in the future

Sloan M. E. Church, Rev. W. H. Jackson, Pastor, 702 Sydnor Street.

Boyington Chapel M. E. Church.

Rev. J. W. Gilder.

1. Herman Griggs
2. Emmerson Norris
3. Willie Brooks
4. Robert French
5. L. G. Alexander
6. Vernon Glover
7. Herman Glover
8. ————
9. Eldridge Jackson
10. John Crowder
11. Harry Huba
12. Mrs. Luella Allen
13. Majorie Wilkerson
14. Sophia Montgomery
15. Nina Smith
16. D. C. Strong
17. Marguerite Williams
18. Arthur Brooun
19. Marion Caldwell
20. Mrs. Florence Sledge
21. Malvena Laave
22. Ruretha Strong
23. Ruth Mathews
24. Eulah Carrington
25. Othella Watkins
26. Ross Bell Carven
27. B. T. Brooks
28. Louise Lights
29. Valree Johnson
30. Wilhelmena Wesley
31. Veoletta Davis
32. Grace Harris
33. Inns Sims
34. Cynthia Watkins
35. Vera Murray

MRS. PEARL AUGUSTA LIGHTS.

Mrs. Pearl Augusta Lights, the beloved daughter of Mr. and Mrs. Commodore Reed, was born June 17th, 1876, at Houston, Texas. Baptized May, 1887, by Father John Yates of Antioch Baptist Church. Married to Dr. F. L. Lights Feb. 11th, 1895. Died Oct. 23rd, 1912. She was a student of Gregory Institute, and after finishing her course was tendered a position in the city schools of Houston, which position she filled until she resigned to become the wife of Dr. F. L. Lights. To this union were born five girls and two boys.

Her life was one of charm, grace and sacredness, ever ready to extend love and sympathy to all. The radiance of her sweet character was reflected in the home among her little ones, and they caught the spirit of the dear mother, early accepting her faith as baptized believers of Antioch Church, thus leading their young lives to her Master, her chief and supreme joy, for she often expressed her love for Christ as being supreme above all else in this world. This inestimable love for Christ gave the incentive to her founding the wish of her life—a nursery for Christ's kingdom. She desired their first impression of life should be of the Savior, the beautiful, true and pure, while their hearts were free from evil. In the fall of 1910, after prayerful consideration, she decided to open a Daily Bible Kindergarten at the Antioch Baptist Church, that the children might be taught Bible stories while engaged in the play work of the kindergarten. She secured the assistance of Mrs. L. H. Spivey, who was formerly Miss Ina Chapman of Mechanicsburg, Ohio, as teacher, and they worked hand in hand. It was largely through her faithfulness and sincerity in the work that the school again opened in the fall of 1911, with an increased attendance. Mrs. Lights' heart's desire was to see a building erected on the Antioch Baptist Church property that would serve as a school and day nursery. It seems the kind Father just waited until her plans were thoroughly ingratiated in the hearts and minds of the people, and then closed her life's work, calling her home to Himself.

The mantle of manager and treasurer seems to have providentially fallen upon Mrs. Venora Allen Bell. Her years of experience in dealing with the little ones and her natural fondness for children particularly fitted her for the position, and she has proven herself an excellent manager, both of the school and funds. Under her management the school has grown from under the Missionary Society to an independent auxiliary or Kindergarten Association. In the fall of 1913, when the school opened, Mrs. Florence McBride-Sledge was elected to fill the vacancy caused by the resignation of Mrs. L. H. Spivey. Mrs. Sledge, a native of Macomb, Illinois, has since her election filled the position with efficiency, doing all in her power to promote the growth of the school, which after five years' existence has all the equipments of a modern kindergarten.

In Memoriam

MRS. F. L. LIGHTS, Deceased.
Born June 17, 1875.   Died October 23, 1912.

Antioch Baptist Church, 311 Robin Street.

REV. F. L. LIGHTS, D. D.

Residence of Rev. N. P. Pullum, 1319 Andrews Street.

Rev. and Mrs. N. P. Pullum.

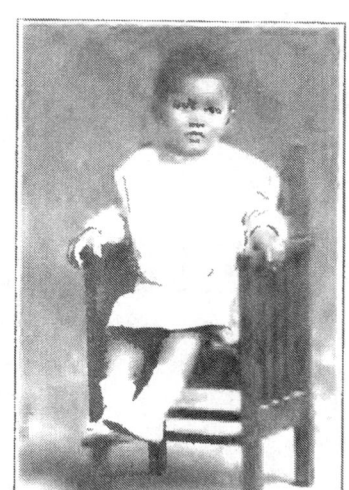

Nathan Lawrence Pullum, Deceased.

Mt. Vernon M. E. Church, 727 Burnett Street.

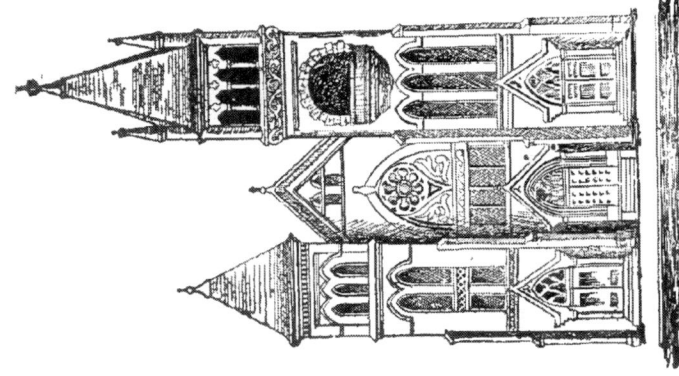

Friendship Baptist Church, corner San Felipe and Heiner.

Fourth Missionary Baptist Church, corner Lamar and Dowling Streets.

Rev. H. B. Southern was born in Washington County in 1869, three and one-half miles from Brenham. He was converted and joined the Ebenezer Baptist Church, Chapel Hill, Texas, in 1887. He was ordained in 1892 and was a student of Theology two years under Dr. J. T. Brown, also took a Theological course at Conroe Normal and Industrial College for two years. He is an author and scholar and has pastored twenty-six churches during his ministry, was missionary and financial secretary of the General Bowen Missionary Baptist Association. He is in his fourth year as pastor of the Fourth Missionary Baptist Church.

Bethel Baptist Church, 801 Andrews Street.

Rev. J. R. Burdett was born in Pilot Point, Texas, in the year of 1878. He is a graduate of Arkansas Baptist College, class of 1911. His property consists of a home in Little Rock, Ark. He was married to Miss Estella Waddy in 1905. Came to Houston in 1915 to pastor the Bethel Baptist Church at 801 Andrews Street. He is a member of R. F. C. and G. U. O. O. F. Pastor at Forest City, Ark., for six years. Missionary work four years. Joined the Baptist Association of Texas.

St. John's Baptist Church, 2104 Broadway.

These cuts represent the St. John Baptist Church on Broadway between Gray and Webster avenues, together with Rev. Wm. Johnson, B.S., D.D., its pastor. St. John is practically a young congregation, having been organized in 1901. This is one of the most important churches of the city. Its seating capacity is practically 1000, and standing room is often at a premium. This church is noted for its attitude toward both civic and benevolent movements in the city and state. The personnel of the congregation is particularly unique, in that it numbers among its membership representatives of practically every calling, profession and avocation in the race, and that the cook, washerwoman, chauffeur, mail carrier, doctor, lawyer, preacher and teacher work and worship side by side without the slightest friction. The motto of this church is: "There can be no failure where there is proper understanding."

Dr. Wm. Johnson, B.S., D.D., is an ex-president of the Mobile Baptist College, and one of the foremost preachers of the age. He is regarded as a deep theologian, versatile writer and brilliant orator. He has filled some of the most popular pulpits of the Baptist denomination, prominent among which are Mount Olive Baptist Church of Opelousas, La., and Franklin Street of Mobile, Ala. He has recently accepted the St. John pastorate, finding when he took charge a membership of 79, which he increased in four months to 450. He is one among that rapidly increasing number of pastors who believe in owning—to use his words "at least a chicken coop on earth before expecting a mansion in Heaven." He owns taxable property in Louisiana, Texas and Alabama. He is married and is educating his children.

Shiloh Baptist Church, Rev. C. W. Holmes, Pastor, 2911 Providence Street.

Mt. Pillar Missionary Baptist Church, Rev. R. L. Williams, Pastor, Hemphill and State Streets.

Wesley A. M. E. Church, 2201 Dowling Street.

Mrs. Mary D. P. Howard.

Rev. Edward James Howard, D. D.

Rev. H. P. Porter, D. D.

Rev. M. C. Brooks.

Bee-Bee Tabernacle C. M. E. Church, corner San Felipe and Arthur Streets.

Rev. W. Q. Hunter, Pastor.

COLORED METHODIST EPISCOPAL CHURCH

The Colored Methodist Episcopal Church is the youngest daughter of Negro Methodism. But her constituents glory in the fact that her ecclesiastical descent can be traced back to the organization of Methodism by John Wesley in 1729, with a broken link, in the great controversy of 1844 which resulted in the division of the Methodist Episcopal Church into two branches, North and South, each branch holding its colored members. At the beginning of the Civil war there were 207,000 colored communicants in the M. E. Church, South. When this great catastrophe (the Civil war) was over, and when the M. E. Church, South, decided at New Orleans in 1866 to organize their colored members into a body separate and distinct from their church, the colored membership had greatly decreased until their numbers were not more than 78,000.

In 1870, according to resolution passed at New Orleans in the General Conference of the M. E. Church, South, in 1866, Bishop Paine, Senior Bishop of the M. E. Church, South, met the colored membership at Jackson, Tenn., in December, 1870, and proceeded to organize the Colored Methodist Episcopal Church. At this meeting W. H. Miles and R. H. Vanderhorst were elected the first bishops of the C. M. E. Church and consecrated by Bishop Paine. Since this time the C. M. E. Church has grown wonderfully.

She now boasts of a membership of 350,000, nine living bishops, three dead, fourteen schools and colleges, one superintendent of missions to Africa, four church papers, a large publishing plant. The C. M. E. Church, though free, separate and distinct in all its governments, the membership from layman to the Bishopric sustains a relation to the Southern white church that no issue or problem has been able to break or mar.

The C. M. E. Church is the only colored Methodist church whose ecclesiastical descent is regular and whose bishops have been regularly elected and consecrated according to the uses and polity of Methodism. "She has gone forth as the brightness of the morning, that shineth more and more unto a perfect day."

REV. H. P. PORTER.
REV. W. G. HUNTER.

REV EDWARD JAMES HOWARD, D D

Edward James Howard, son of Edward and Mary Howard, was born December 25, 1870, at Boonville, Cooper County, Missouri   His parents moved to Paola, Miami County, Kansas, in the spring of 1875   His education was begun in the Paola High School.   He learned the trade of plasterer under his father   Converted at the age of twelve years, he joined the A M E Church and grew up as an active member of the same, serving as steward and Sunday School teacher   He was married to Miss Mary Dallas Partilla, June 27, 1894, at Spring Hill, Kansas   He experienced a call to the Christian ministry in 1896, and was licensed to preach during the same year   He came to Waco, Texas, in 1897, and was appointed pastor of St Luke Mission in East Waco   The membership was then only eight in number   He was ordained deacon under the missionary rule in November 1897, at Cameron, Texas, by Bishops A Grant and J H Armstrong   From this conference he was appointed to Cox Providence and Little Rocky Circuit, where he built a three-room parsonage   In the fall of 1896 he was appointed to Taylor Circuit   He remained here four years, rebuilt the church   remodeled the parsonage and increased the membership from 20 to 160   He was appointed to Temple Texas, in the fall of 1902   Here he paid for ground previously purchased, and built a five-room parsonage   He remained here two years   His next appointment was to El Paso, Texas   He remained at El Paso four years   He increased the membership from 60 to 150, paid a mortgage debt of $500 00, bought three lots at a cost of $1,200 00, and built a red pressed brick church at a cost of $13,000 00   He was returned to Waco and stationed at St Paul   Here he paid a mortgage debt of $468 00 paid a balance of $2,000 00 on property bought for a new church site, and built the best church of the connection in the Southwest   In the fall of 1914 he was transferred from the Central Texas Conference to the Texas Conference and stationed at Wesley Chapel, Houston   Many conversions and accessions have marked all his pastorates   While at Waco he took up special study at Paul Quinn College   It was this institution that conferred upon him the degree of Doctor of Divinity   He has been a member of the Board of Trustees and the Executive Board of Paul Quinn College for seven years   He is well known in church circles of his State and is beloved by all his brethren

He was a delegate to the General Conference of his church that met in Kansas City in 1912, leading his delegation from the Central Texas Conference   He now represents the Tenth Episcopal District on the Financial Board

It is noteworthy to say just here that circumstances prevented the rounding out of an education as he so desired, but by his dynamic will power and tact he has stood always with men who were his intellectual superiors, and is felt among his people because of the unstinted service and love for humanity   Wherever he has gone to carry the gospel he has endeavored to help his people be their best and do their best   Another thing that shows the big heart of the man is his unselfish way of dealing with his fellow brethren of all denominations   He served as President of the Ministers Union in Waco, and is acting in the same capacity now in Houston   We can readily see that his labors are not for self-aggrandizement or glory, but rather to help in the great plan of lifting up his belated black brother   Aside from his sincerity, honesty and devotion in his work another thing that makes him succeed is his willingness to let every member in his church do something, both little and big, and greatest of all, he never attempts to monopolize the honor for things done to himself, but rather pays the tribute to those faithful followers   He moves in and out among his people with an unassuming gentility that draws the young and aspiring and the old and retired alike   In this short sketch we cannot add or detract from the name or work of Rev Howard   We simply pronounce the name and relate the work and leave them shining on, rejoicing that he still lives by the side of the way to be a friend to man

J. J. HARDEWAY.

J. J. Hardeway was born Oct. 25th, 1868, in Polk County, Texas, on a farm. He left the farm at the age of 18 and taught school eleven years, at and near Livingston, Texas, in his home county. After quitting the teaching profession of his own accord, he was the owner and manager of a store of general merchandise for four years. He moved to Houston, Texas, Jan. 1st, 1903, and represented an insurance company for about three years. Then he established the Real Estate and Rental business, in which he has been continuously engaged for more than nine years. He has been a Notary Public since June 1st, 1907. He married Miss Dora Ann Freeman in 1888, with whom he lived until she was taken away on Dec. 26th, 1914. Their union was blessed with six children, namely: O. R., R. D., C. R., R. S., J. L. and Miss Piccola Ruth, all of whom are living. He is a member, steward and trustee of Trinity M. E. Church; member of the F. B of F. and A. O. of P. He owns stock in an old-line insurance company, in a drug store, and owns some real estate in and near Houston, Texas.

Rev. and Mrs. J. A. Pendleton.

The above cut is that of Elder James Pendleton and his wife, Lillie Bell Price Pendleton. This happy couple were united in the holy bonds of matrimony in Houston, Texas, June 25, 1913, in the Church of God, corner Sherman and Saulnier Streets, of which Elder Pendleton is pastor. It is generally considered that the Pendleton-Price wedding was among the most important that Houston has produced, being attended by white and colored en masse. Elder Pendleton is the founder of the Church of God in Houston; starting without a single member or one foot of ground, in six years he had purchased a lot for $600.00 and had erected a beautiful church building and a hall for amusement purposes at an expense of $2,000.00; every cent being paid on property and buildings in six years. The membership of this church runs into the hundreds. Besides being the pastor of the Houston Temple, Elder Pendleton is the pastor of the Church of God at Galveston, Texas, and is chairman of the General Assembly of the Church of God. Aside from his district ministerial work, Elder Pendleton and Mrs. Lillie Bell Pendleton are the editor and editress, respectively, of the Church of God Review, a religious periodical published semi-monthly, at 419½ Milam Street, Houston, Texas. Being launched on February 21, 1911, this religious periodical has grown by leaps and by bounds, being increased in size three times in four years. The Church of God Review is the official organ of the church, and is particularly adapted to religious matter. Since their marriage the Pendletons have resided continuously at 319 San Felipe street.

In Memoriam

PROF. J. M. CODWELL, Deceased.
Born 1865   Died 1911.

RISE OF THE RACE

POPULATION.

While the population of the Afro-American race in the United States is not increasing as fast as that of the white race, still it has increased 150 per cent in the past fifty years. The population, estimated in round numbers, at the close of the war was four million, and it is now about ten million. It has increased for the last twenty years at the rate of one hundred thousand per year.

PERCENTAGE OF POPULATION.

In 1870 the Afro-American race composed 15 per cent of the whole inhabitants of the United States, while today it only comprises 11 per cent of the whole. This disproportionate showing is due, not to a difference in natural increase of the races, but to the larger immigration of the white races and the almost entire lack of immigration from African countries. To give a resume of this would take up too much space for this article.

The population is distributed by States as follows:

Less than 1 per cent of the population of Washington, Idaho, Oregon, California, Nevada, Utah, New Mexico, Montana, North and South Dakota, Nebraska, Minnesota, Iowa, Wisconsin, Michigan, Maine, Vermont and New Hampshire is African.

From 1 to 5 per cent of the entire population of the following States is Afro-American: Arizona, Colorado, Wyoming, Kansas, Missouri, Illinois, Indiana, Ohio, Pennsylvania, New York, Massachusetts, Connecticut, Rhode Island and New Jersey.

The following States have an Afro-American population of from 5 to $12\frac{1}{2}$ per cent of the whole: Oklahoma, Kentucky, West Virginia. Texas, Tennessee, Maryland and Delaware have from $12\frac{1}{2}$ to 25 per cent Afro-American population. In three States the percentage of Afro-American population ranges from 25 to $37\frac{1}{2}$ per cent of the whole; these are Arkansas, Virginia and North Carolina.

In four States the Afro-American population ranges from $37\frac{1}{2}$ to 50 per cent. These are Louisiana, Alabama, Georgia and Florida. Only in two States of the Union have the Afro-Americans a population of over 50 per cent of the whole. These are Mississippi and South Carolina.

Taking the population by States for the seven States with largest Afro-American percentage, the following are the figures given by the last United States census: Georgia, 1,176,987; Mississippi, 1,009,487; Alabama, 908,282; South Carolina, 835,843; Louisiana, 713,874; North Carolina, 697,853; Texas, 690,049.

To these figures may be added about $2\frac{1}{2}$ per cent, as that increase is evident since the 1910 census was brought out.

The Afro-American race in the United States shows a smaller rate of foreign born than any other race or people, less than one out of 200 being the percentage of foreign born   Taking all other races together to make the figures for the white races, one in eight is foreign born

The Afro-Americans in Texas may be set down now at 700,000, which is an increase of 210,000 since 1890, or an increase of 2 per cent per year for twenty years

WEALTH

On the other hand the increase in wealth has been gratifying, when the handicaps under which the race operated are taken into consideration   At the close of the war the uncertain census returns gave the wealth of the race at about $20,000,000 00 It certainly did not go over $25,000 000 00   At the close of this fifty-year period, it has reached a sum in excess of $700,000,000 00   Some authorities claim it reaches the billion dollar mark, and some estimate it as low as a half billion   A safe figure to place it at now, from all the obtainable data, is $725,000,000 00   This means that while the race has only increased 150 per cent in population, the wealth of the race has increased 2,900 per cent It is probable at the close of the war that the greater majority of this wealth was in agricultural lands, and the same holds good now   The value represented by farm lands and farm implements and improvements reaches well above the $400,000,000 00 mark, and the remainder of the sum is in real estate, houses and establishments in the cities Of course, compared with the overwhelming increase in wealth of the American race, it appears only a small sum, still it represents a greater progress economically, industrially and from the standpoint of accumulation than that made by any race that has come up out of slavery in the first fifty years of its emancipation   The wealth of the race is something over $70 per capita, and this is by far the best record made by a race during the first fifty years of its economic existence   A reference to this fact is seen in Emmett J Scott's article in this book on "Efficiency"   While the per capita just after the war was under $6, today it is twelve times as great   The average of wealth for each one of the 10,000,000 is thirteen times greater than the average of the 4,000,000 in 1870

FARMS

Of the total number of owner-operated farms in Texas, nearly 22,000, or one-eighth of the owners who operate their farms, are Afro-Americans   It is impossible to estimate the acreage of these 22,000 farms, but the significant fact is presented that over three-fourths of these farms are reported out of debt, while less than two-thirds of those owned and operated by the white farmers are out of debt   Of the total number of rented farms in the State, about 50,000, or one-third, are rented by Afro-Americans   Of the managed farms nearly 100 have Afro-American managers

Taking the whole Texas farm situation, both owner-operated and rented, nearly one-fourth of the farmers are Afro-Americans   It is impossible to give the value of the acreage owned by members of the race, as such statistics are unavailable   However, reports from 3,200 of such farms give an average of $1 750 valuation each If this average be maintained throughout the entire number of farms owned by members of the race in Texas, it would show a total of $38 000 000 00

HARRIS COUNTY FARMS

Of the less than 1,600 farms cultivated in Harris County over one-fourth are operated by Afro-Americans   Of these 50 per cent are owners and 7 per cent managers, the rest being renters

FARMS IN UNITED STATES

The total number of farms owned, managed and rented in the United States in 1910 is given as 893,370, which is an increase in number for the ten years prior of 146,655. If this same increase ratio has held until now, the number of such is over 900,000.

OWNERS

The number owning their farms is given as 218,972, which is an increase of 20 per cent in ten years. The same increase holding good, would make the number of farm owners now about 240,000.

ACREAGE

The total farm acreage estimated from the census is over 46,000,000 acres.

VALUE

The total value of farm property owned or operated by Afro-Americans in the United States is given by the 1910 census as $1,141,792,526. According to the percentage of increase for the ten years prior this value should now be about $1,870,000,000.

DISTRIBUTION

This value is distributed by States in those States having $3,000,000 worth of property or more as follows (the figures given after each State are in millions of dollars): Alabama, 77, Arkansas, 71, Florida, 12, Georgia, 133, Illinois, 6, Indiana, 3, Kansas, 7, Kentucky, 15, Louisiana, 46, Maryland 10, Mississippi, 153, Missouri, 12, North Carolina, 69, Ohio, 6, Oklahoma, 25, South Carolina, 102, Tennessee, 44, Texas, 93, Virginia, 47.

FOR TEXAS

The number of farms in Texas owned or operated by Afro-Americans is now over 70,000. Of these over 21,000 are owners and about 50,000 are tenants or managers.

Texas is fourth in value of farm properties, and is second in number of farms owned. Virginia comes first in number of farms owned with nearly 33,000. Texas is, however, far behind the other Southern States in the percentage of increase in farm ownership, standing twenty-fourth in the number of States. As to number of total Afro-American population by States, Texas stands seventh.

POPULATION

The total Afro-American population of United States and possessions is given as follows. United States proper, 9,827,763, Alaska, 209, Hawaii, 695, and Porto Rico, 386,437, a total of over ten million. The Afro-Americans have increased during the last decade at the rate of over 11 per cent. The increase of the white population during that period has been over 22 per cent. This greater percentage of increase of whites is due, however, mostly to immigration. The increase of the Afro-American race is due almost entirely to natural increase of births over deaths, as only an incomparable per cent is due to immigration.

CENTER OF POPULATION

The center of Afro-American population is now in the northeast corner of Alabama, near the town of Fort Payne. The center of population in 1790 was in the southeastern portion of Virginia. This center has since traveled in a direction southwest by west until it is where stated, having moved a distance of about 485 miles since 1790 In another ten or twenty years it will be near the corners of Tennessee, Alabama and Mississippi, if the present trend is continued

The population of the United States proper, by decades

CENSUS YEAR	POPULATION AT EACH CENSUS, 1790 1910				
	Total	Negro		White	Indian, Chinese, Japanese, and all other
		Number	Per cent		
1910	91,972,266	9,827,763	10 7	81,731,957	412,546
1900	75,994,575	8,833,994	11 6	66,809,196	351,385
1890	62,947,714	7,488,676	11 9	55,101,258	356,780
1880	50,155,783	6,580,793	13 1	43,402,970	172,020
1870	39,818,449	5 392,172	13 5	34,337 292	88,985
1860	31,443 321	4,441,830	14 1	26,922,537	78,954
1850	23 191,876	3,638,808	15 7	19,553,068	
1840	17,069,453	2,873,648	16 8	14,195,805	
1830	12,866,020	2,328,642	18 1	10,537,378	
1820	9,638,153	1,771,656	18 4	7,866,797	
1810	7,239,881	1,377,808	19 0	5,862,073	
1800	5 308 483	1,002,037	18 9	4 306,416	
1790	3 929,214	757 208	19 3	3 172,006	

URBAN AND RURAL POPULATION

In 1910 the percentage of Afro-Americans living in rural communities was 72 6, the remainder living in towns and cities

The Afro-Americans represent 14 5 per cent of the total rural population of the country and 6 3 per cent of the city population

The following table gives the 43 cities of the United States having a population of ten thousand or more Afro-Americans

CITY	POPULATION		INCREASE *	
	1910	1900	Number	Per cent
Washington, D C	94,446	86,702	7,744	8 9
New York, N Y	91,709	60,666	31,043	51 2
New Orleans, La	89 262	77,714	11 548	14 9
Baltimore, Md	84,749	79 258	5,491	6 9
Philadelphia, Pa	84,459	62,613	21,846	34 9
Memphis, Tenn	52,441	49,910	2,531	5 1
Birmingham, Ala	52,305	16,575	35,730	215 6
Atlanta, Ga	51,902	35,727	16,175	45 3
Richmond, Va	46,733	32,230	14,503	45 0
Chicago, Ill	44,103	30,150	13,953	46 3
St Louis, Mo	43,960	35,516	8,444	23 8
Louisville, Ky	40,522	39,139	1,383	3 5
Nashville, Tenn	36,523	30,044	6,479	21 6
Savannah, Ga	33,246	28,090	5,156	18 4
Charleston, S C	31 056	31,522	—466	—1 5
Jacksonville, Fla	29,293	16,236	13,057	80 4
Pittsburgh, Pa	25 623	20,355	5,268	25 9
Norfolk, Va	25,039	20,230	4,809	23 8
Houston, Tex	23,929	14 608	9,321	63 8

* A minus sign (—) denotes decrease

URBAN AND RURAL POPULATION—Continued

CITY	POPULATION		INCREASE *	
	1910	**1900**	Number	Per cent
Kansas City, Mo	23,566	17,567	5,999	31 1
Mobile, Ala	22,763	17,045	5,718	33 5
Indianapolis, Ind	21,816	15,931	5,885	36 9
Cincinnati, Ohio	19,639	14,482	5,157	35 6
Montgomery, Ala	19,322	17,229	2,093	12 1
August, Ga	18,344	18,487	—113	—0 8
Macon, Ga	18,150	11,550	6,600	57 1
Dallas, Tex	18,024	9,035	8,989	99 5
Chattanooga, Tenn	17,942	13,122	4,820	36 7
Little Rock, Ark	14,539	14,694	—155	—1 1
Shreveport, La	13,896	8,512	5,354	62 7
Boston Miss	13,564	11,591	1,973	17 0
Ft Worth, Tex	13,280	4,219	9,031	212 5
Columbus, Ohio	12 739	8,201	4,538	55 3
Wilmington, N C	12,107	10,107	1,700	16 3
Vicksburg, Miss	12,053	8,147	3,906	47 9
Charlotte N C	11,752	7,151	1,601	64 3
Portsmouth, Va	11,617	5,625	5,992	106 5
Columbia, S C	11,646	9,858	1,688	17 1
Petersburg, Va	11,014	10,751	263	2 4
Lexington Ky	11,011	10,130	881	8 7
San Antonio, Tex	10,716	7,538	3,178	12 2
Jackson, Miss	10 554	4 447	6 107	137 3
Pensacola Fla	10 214	8,561	1,653	19 3

* A minus sign (—) denotes decrease

HOME OWNERS IN CITIES

Houston is fourteenth in the number of homes with 5,800 and ninth in the number of homes owned with 1,183   Baltimore, with 18,000 homes, reports only 933 as owned   Louisville, with a total of 11,000 homes, reports only 711 owned   New Orleans has the largest number reported, being 21,880, with 2,431 owned   Washington, with an Afro-American population of nearly 95,000 souls, reports only 2,072 homes, with only 737 owned   There is no way of determining the value of these owned homes as no record has been kept by the United States census department

HOMES BOTH RURAL AND URBAN

Texas is sixth in the number of homes reported with 145 890   It is second in the number of homes owned with 41,583   Of these the number free from debt is given as 31,607

Taking the Southern States, with a population in 1910 of 8,749,427, which is an increase of 836,458, we have a total number of homes of 1,917,391, an increase in the number of homes in the prior ten years of 280,367, or over 28,000 per year for ten years

The total of these homes owned is given as 430,449   Of these owned homes 314,340 are reported free from debt

Of the above number of total homes, 864,688 are farm homes, of these the total owned is 212,508, an increase in the number of farm homes owned of 18 per cent in the prior ten years   The total number of homes other than farm homes is given as 1,052,703 and the number owned is given as 217,942, which is an increase of 40 per cent over 1900   The number of owned homes free from debt in. 1910 is given as 162 293, which is an increase of 60 per cent of homes owned free from debt over 1900

In the Southern States 77 per cent of the homes owned are free from mortgage or incumbrance

PERCENTAGE OF BLACK AND MULATTO

The following table gives the classification of the Afro-American race in the United States, divided as to Blacks and Mulattoes

CENSUS YEAR	POPULATION			PER CENT	
	Total	Black*	Mulatto*	Black	Mulatto
1910	9,827,763	7,777,077	2 050,686	79 1	20 9
1900	8 843 994				
1890	†7,488,676	6,337,980	1,132 060	84 8	15 2
1880	6,580,793				
1870	4,880 009	1,295,960	584,049	88 0	12 0
1860	4 441,830	3 853,467	588 363	86 8	13 2
1850	3,638,808	3 233,057	405,751	88 8	11 2

* No data for 1880 or 1900
† Includes 18,636 Negroes enumerated in Indian Territory, not distinguished as black or mulatto

RELIGIOUS BODIES, ETC

The following summary was taken from the religious census taken by the United States Census Department in 1906.

Organizations	36 770
Communicants or members	3,685 097
Places of worship	
Church edifices	35,160
Halls, etc	1 261
Seating capacity of church edifices	10 481 738
Parsonages	4,779
Value of church property	
Church edifices	$56,637,159
Parsonages	$3 727,884
Debt on church property	$5,005,905
Sunday Schools	
Number of schools	34,681
Officers and teachers	210 148
Scholars	1,740,009

From 1890 to 1906 the Afro-American population increased 26 1 per cent, while during the same period the number of church organizations increased 56 7 per cent and the number of communicants increased 37 8 per cent, the number of church edifices increased 47 9 per cent, the seating capacity increased 54 1 per cent

According to the increase shown in the above statement, taking the table as it stands today, the probable membership of the several denominations is something like four and a quarter million

South Carolina is first in church membership with a total of over half a million communicants and Texas comes seventh with nearly a quarter of a million

The figures as given in the tables compiled in Bulletin 129, Census Department give the communicants for the several denominations as follows Those of Baptist faith, 2,354,789 Of these two and one-half million belong to the National Baptist Convention

Next come the Methodists with a membership of 1,181,131, the A M E with 494,777, the M E's with 308 551, the A M E Z's with 184,542 and the C M E Church with 172,996 members

PERCENTAGE OF COMMUNICANTS TO POPULATION

The population of the United States (Afro-American) was given for 1910 as 4,885,-881 males, and 4,941,882 females Of these 1,373,954 males were under ten years old and 1,388,273 females were under ten years old

This gives a total population of 7,065,536 over ten years old Taking the number of communicants as given by the above table and not allowing for the probable increase in percentage of communicants we have over 52 per cent of the population over ten years old as members of the different churches

The figures in this article were compiled from Bulletin No 129 and the statistics given in that are taken from reports from sixteen denominations composed wholly of Afro-American church organizations and twenty-six denominations composed both of white and Afro-American church organizations

DR FREDERICK L LIGHTS

Dr Lights, Baptist minister, residing at 819 Andrews Street, phone Preston 5531 He is president of the Foreign Mission Convention of Texas, President of the General Board of Trustees of Missionary and Educational Convention, Treasurer of Old Land Mark Association, the Eminent Pastor of the Antioch Baptist Church of Houston, and President of the Ministers Alliance of Houston

F L Lights is in the front rank of the Baptist preachers Born in Louisiana July 4th, 1859 At the age of twelve his father, Rev F L Lights, Sr, brought him to Texas and located at Bryan, Texas, where he attended the city school After the death of his father he was compelled to work during the day and go to school at night Later, feeling a divine call to preach the gospel, he was among the first to enroll as a student in Hearne Academy at Hearne, Texas

He was a hard worker careful and exact and did not hesitate to apply himself closely to the studies of the course in order to acquire an education He was converted at Bryan, Texas, in the Shiloh Baptist Church under the pastorage of Rev A T Thompson in 1875 This church was organized by his father He was ordained at the Pleasant Grove Baptist Church at Edge, Texas, August 11, 1882

He has pastored some of our best churches, such as Bryan, Hearne, Franklin, Bremond, Cameron, Rockdale, Hempstead, Hammon Colony, Allen Farm and Wellburn, Tex He has built respectable houses of worship The Franklin Grove, Wheelock, Pleasant Grove, Edge, Cameron Grove at Cameron He built two meeting houses at Hempstead, enlarged the Baptist meeting house at Hearne, completed the meeting house at Bremond, completed the meeting house at Canaan near Bryan, enlarged and completed the Baptist meeting house at Houston, has built up the denomination to permanence wherever his lot was cast as pastor He has baptized more than 5,000 converts, married more than a thousand couples, preached the funerals of hundreds of the saints to the comfort of the hearts of the mourners As a pastor Dr Lights has won the hearts of all his auditors and the friendship of all denominations He is a household ideal in every community and city wherever he has preached He has been interested in all the enterprises for the uplift of his people

Dr Lights has traveled extensively abroad He was messenger to the World's Baptist Congress in 1905 While in Europe he visited in England, Ireland and Scotland In 1910 he went to the World's Foreign Mission Congress, which was at Edinburgh, Scotland, where all the religious denominations of the world were represented He again took side trips to France, Belgium, Germany and Wales

The National Baptist Convention met in Houston according to his invitation in 1912 It was just one month after the National Convention met that Mrs Pearl Augusta Lights, truly the helpmeet of Dr Lights, his amiable wife and angel, was summoned to her rest There never was a more helpful minister's wife than Mrs Lights Her good work will live on through ages

It has been said that Louisiana never gave birth to a nobler character than F L Lights He has often been referred to as the model pastor of Texas For truth and veracity he can be relied upon Any person will testify to his moral standing He is always willing to subordinate ambition to serve his race Dr Light's influence will live long after he has gone to his reward

New Mt. Pilgrim Baptist Church, Rev. Wash Rhodes, Pastor, 3405 St. Charles Street.

REV. N. P. PULLUM.

Rev. N. P. Pullum was born at Pickingsville, La., in 1862. Attended school at Corinth, Miss., and Pastor's School in Tuscaloosa, Ala., and Selma, La. Became a member of the Baptist Church in 1887 and two years later was publicly ordained to the ministry by a council of nine messengers from ten churches. The council was composed of John C. Crawford, W. A. Shelby, Elder P. Murrell, Solomon Page, A. J. Austin, J. M. Mason, T. Dinon, J. W. White and J. M. Sewell. Married in 1881 to Miss Lizzie Mustin, who died four years later. Married in 1890 to Miss Emma Chandler. Rev. Pullum pastored in Louisiana from 1889 to 1895, holding three pastorates during that time. Came to Texas in 1895, when he was called to the Antioch Baptist Church at Beaumont. In 1898 he accepted the charge of the Bethel Baptist Church at Houston and remained in this work for five years. He then resigned and accepted the call to the Friendship Baptist Church in 1903 and is still engaged in this work. Under his administration the church bought a lot now valued at about $5,000 and started the erection of a twenty thousand dollar church edifice. The first story of the church is completed and furnished for holding services. Rev. Pullum has long been interested in the uplift of his people and has engaged in other pursuits to help out his work. He is proprietor of the Pullum Brick Yards and has accumulated during his work in Houston property, including homestead, lots, etc., to the amount of nearly forty thousand dollars. He is a member of K. of P. and Masons. His residence is at 1319 Andrews Street; phone Preston 302.

St. Paul A. M. E. Church, Rev. J. L. Mosely, Pastor, 1710 Edwards Street.

REV. JESSE W. GILDER.

Rev. Jesse W. Gilder was born at Concord, a suburban village near Beaumont, Jefferson County, Texas, on or about the 15th of August, 1871. When two months old his mother, who had been a young slave, moved to Beaumont, Texas, where he was reared to manhood. Reading, writing and arithmetic, taught to the tune of a hickory stick, made their first impressions on his young mind and back in the public schools of Beaumont. His parents being very poor and unable to continue him in school, he was forced, by reason of circumstances, to leave home at a very early age to shift for himself. Like most boys who drift, he found himself surrounded by evil companions. Strange as it may seem, he never became addicted to the use of tobacco, liquor, or to gambling. He was often abused and sometimes beaten because he refused to join his companions in things of a criminal nature. Rev. Gilder attributes this to the early training in the home by a Christian mother and the lessons learned in the Sunday School. Being religiously inclined from a child, endowed with natural gifts of intelligence and common sense, he applied himself to his studies under private instructors, trying to fit himself for the battle of life. Quite fifteen years ago he became conscious of a call to the ministry, but was seven years trying to get the consent of his mind to enter, but finally entered quite eight years ago, having joined the Texas Conference of the Methodist Episcopal Church at Paris, Texas, November, 1908, was received by Bishop William A. Quayle. Rev. Gilder has served successfully from the country mission and circuit to his present charge (Boynton Chapel), which is one of the best city charges in the Conference, where he is serving his third year successfully. Besides this he is first assistant treasurer of the Conference, chairman of the Board on Conference Relation, and at present secretary of the Interdenominational Ministers' Union of the City of Houston, Texas.

REV. M. E. ROBINSON.

Rev. M. E. Robinson is a native of Polk County, Texas, born in 1868. Residence, 910 Schwartz Street, which he owns. Residence phone, Preston 8119. Rev. Robinson is a graduate of Conroe Normal and Industrial College. Was married to Miss Mella Brooks in 1887. He is a member of White Rock Baptist Church. He was converted in 1884 and ordained in 1892. He has been pastor of Antioch Baptist Church of Beaumont 14 years and of Providence Baptist Church, Leggett, Texas, 7 years. He is the founder of the Beaumont Normal and Industrial College of Beaumont, Texas. Served as Moderator of the General Bowen's Baptist Association 14 years, is now President of the Baptist State Convention of Texas and Vice-President of the National Baptist Convention of U. S. A.

HOUSTON CHURCHES

THE ANTIOCH BAPTIST CHURCH

Was organized on the second Lord's day in January, 1866, by Rev. Mr. Crane, a white minister and missionary of the State of Texas at that time. The following persons participated in the organization: John Wheeler, Henry Styles, Edward Smith, Preston Greenhill, Daniel Riley, T. L. Brown, Sandy Parker, Wash Rhodes, Isaac Williams, Rhyna Moore, Margaret Jones and Cynthia Hill.

From January to August of this year, this band of Christian workers had no place in which to worship other than the privilege granted them by the First Baptist (white) and the German Baptist (white) to use their churches.

On the first Lord's day in August, 1866, Rev. I. S. Campbell and Rev. I. Rhinehart reorganized the church and gave it the name it now bears. Rev. Campbell served as pastor until the fall of 1868, when Rev. Jack Yates was ordained and chosen as pastor.

Since the organization of Antioch Baptist Church 48 years ago, there has only been two real active pastors—Rev. Jack Yates and its present pastor, Rev. Fred Lee Lights. Rev. Yates served 24 years, and Rev. Lights is now serving his 21st year.

The church remained without a pastor from 1891 to 1894, during which time the management was under the direct supervision of the Deacon Board. In the meantime, though, two pastors were chosen—Rev. Peter Diggs of Texas and Rev. White of North Carolina, neither of whom accepted the responsibility.

The present pastor, Rev. F. L. Lights, was chosen January 29, 1894, and accepted the call the second Sunday in March, the same year. There has been a sure and steady growth since 1894, gradually and constantly casting off the old habiliments, the old ideas, forms and customs, until today it shines in effulgent rays, resplendent with victory, shedding peace, happiness, influence and love into every nook and corner.

On account of the splendid management of affairs, the church enjoys the confidence of the entire citizenship of this city and state. It points with pride to the organization of all its forces, to the discipline maintained, to the amount of spiritual work, and to the proper safeguarding of all finances. Its reputation is that it gives as much thought and consideration to a one-cent piece as to the $1.00 bill.

The membership—active—is about 1684. In 1894 it was 319.

The following is a statement of the amount of spiritual and financial work done. From 1895 to 1905, inclusive, there are no available records which will assist in determining the total accessions to the church, but for other years it is as follows:

1894	1906	1907	1908	1909	1910	1911	1912	1913	1914	Total
153	140	414	155	141	126	107	229	151	214	1830

	Total
Total received by baptism	743
Total received by experience	310
Total received by restoration	234
Total received by letter	151
Total received by watch care	392
Total	1830

For the ten years an average of 183 members per year, and if this average is applied to the eleven years unaccounted for the accessions would have been something like 3840

FINANCES

The church has in the last sixteen years collected $68,922 38

An average yearly receipt of $4,307 65

An average monthly receipt of $358 97

This enormous sum, or the greater part, was spent for foreign missions, home and state missions, educational work, charity, and improvements on the church building

The church has all the modern equipment—two baptizing pools, electric lights and fans, heating system, sanitary connections and pipe organ

The auxiliaries are the W M S, the Sunday School, B Y P U and kindergarten classes

Present Officers F L Lights, pastor; W E Miller, church clerk

Deacons W E Jones, Starkey Watson, J D Collins, W E Brooks, D D Carter, W H Hogan, Jas A Prater, Alex Hood, J B Bell, Sam Tate, W H Parker, L H Spivey, E D Pierson and W E Miller

Trustees John L Gray, Chas Payne, Dan Hood, E R Moore and Horace Hicks

BETHEL BAPTIST CHURCH

Corner Crosby and Andrews Streets Organized in September, 1891 First pastor, Rev Jack Yates Other pastors Revs N P Pullum J J Blackshear, J E Knox and C C Harper. Charter members now living and in the church, about 25 Present membership, 640 1914 was a most successful year under present pastor, C C Harper, who raised $5,000 00 and added 300 members in fifteen months Present ordained deacons J Perry, Jas Kinsey Tom Jones, A Lacey, Joe Sigh, A D Paley, C Fulcher Trustees M Smith, J H Harmon, L G Alexander, R B H Yates, W E Green Church clerk, E S McCullough

BOYNTON CHAPEL A M E CHURCH

1120 Paige Street, was organized in 1885 by Rev Porter Bush and named in honor of Bishop Boynton, who donated the property For the past three years the church has been under the pastorate of Rev J W Gilder, and during that time has grown from a rating of 6 to that of 1 Plans are being considered for a new enlarged church edifice Present membership 300

MT VERNON M E CHURCH

Mount Vernon Methodist Episcopal Church, corner Clark and Burnett Streets, Houston Texas, was organized in 1870 and was then located on Vine Street and was known as Union Church, because both Methodists and Baptists worshiped there The Methodists had two Sundays in the month and the Baptists two, but the congregation was made up of both denominations whenever the church was open for services Later the church took the name of Toby's Church, because the land on which it was situated was purchased by Uncle Toby, who had lived on a part of it

More than three thousand souls have come to Christ through the influence of this organization   The following is the list of pastors who have been appointed to this charge in consecutive order

Rev Bryant was the first, who was succeeded by Rev W W Brown, and then came Revs V M Cole Paul Douglass, Spencer Hardwell, J S Whittaker. W B Pullam, Jesse Shackelford, Tenola Edwards R R Roberts, Isom Snell, C C Minegan (twice), Freeman Parker (twice) Edward Lee, H S McMillan, William Wesley, P H Jenkins, J O Williams, Frank Gary, W A Fortson, K W McMillan, and the present pastor, Rev J I Gilmore

The church edifice on Vine Street was destroyed by the storm of 1900, at an approximate loss of $5,000 00 to the membership   It was immediately rebuilt on the present site, Burnett and Clark and today the church property is valued at $6,000 00 and the parsonage at $1,800 00, all of which is unincumbered

The present membership is four hundred fifty-one (451)   All of the auxiliaries are organized and well intact   A special fund is set aside to relieve the wants of the sick the poor and the distressed

PAYNE CHAPEL

Payne Chapel A M E Church, Hill Street, Fifth Ward, was organized some time during 1886 by Rev Richard Green

The present membership is 60   Number of officers are 9 trustees, 9 stewards, 9 stewardesses, 6 class leaders

The corner-stone was laid in 1907 by the Summer Lodge, No 4021, G U O of O F

Trustees   Jas Franklin, Wm Hackney Deal Crawford, G W Tyrons Chas Skinner Wm Crawford, A Byons, Jas Porter, and Rev J B Butler, pastor

Present pastor and officers   Rev O L Bonner Wm Hackney, Harrison Marbury, John Walker, J P Price, Ed James Wm Crawford, L S Tharpe, G W Tyrons, Geo Cornish

Stewardesses   Mesdames Lucy Crawford, Estella Tharpe Narcis Richardson, M F Stafford, V M Franklin Henretta Walker Mary Stevenson, Annie Fifer, Annie Woodards

SHILOH BAPTIST CHURCH

Organized in 1900 by present pastor, Rev C W Holmes B D , with a membership of 96   The first congregation met in a little unfinished frame building   During the incumbency of the pastor who organized the church and who is still with his people, the church has erected a large stone church edifice costing $10,000 00 and the membership has grown to 500   Board of Deacons   S Williams, G W Thomas, Taylor Clark, R L Holmes, C Pollard, W T Vincent F I Richardson, W J Henry, S Houston, J Stanley

BEE BEE TABERNACLE C M E CHURCH
(Originally Sherman Chapel)

Organized in 1890   The church was blown down in 1900 and rebuilt in 1902   The church was named in honor of Bishop BeeBee   Present pastor, Rev W Q Hunter

SLOAN MEMORIAL METHODIST EPISCOPAL CHURCH.

Known in its early history as the Sloan Street Church, was organized in 1870 by Rev Ed Roscoe, a local deacon, assisted by Revs George Davis and James Smith Its first trustees were Charles Nickerson Enoch Sherman, Richard (Dick) Thomas Wash Breed, Louis V Evans and Steve Marshall

The church has had a stormy period trying to lay a deep foundation and striving to step into prominence and it took years for it to get into line as a prominent church

The church has been served by the following pastors Revs Ed Roscoe Fletcher Norwood, Ed Harris, John L Smith, G J Izzard, Jesse Jones, H R Smith Wade Hamilton, D D, C G Curtis, W B Pullam, Benjamin Manning Taylor, W L Duncan, David C Harley, D D, Freeman Parker, D D, G E D Belcher, and W Hartley Jackson, D D editor Taborian Banner and Navasota Bugle

The present board of trustees is composed of the following W W Ballard, president, Sam Cebron, secretary, Mrs Delia L Jones, treasurer, Wm O'Neil, Milton Wright Prince Lampkins, Joe Palmer. O D Hall and W H Montgomery Stewards A Harvey, Thomas Hogan, W W Ballard Leon Wilson W H Montgomery, Alex Nelson O D Hall, Harrison Jones W Miller D L Jones, M E Mitchell and Sam Cebron, R S Local preachers Wilson Miller and R N Overton Class leaders O D Hall, J Palmer, Tillie Stelivan, D L Jones, S Cebron, Nettie Smith, Joe Greene, Allen Johnson, Thos Hogan, Turner Eldridge, Leon Wilson Alex Nelson, Moses Maas B J Williams and M E Mitchell

THE FOURTH MISSIONARY BAPTIST CHURCH

The Fourth Missionary Baptist Church known as Watts Chapel, was organized December 29 1883, by Rev Henry Watts, pastor, assisted by Dr J M C Breaker of white Baptist church, Rev Joe Robinson and Deacon Josh Watson of the Antioch Baptist Church

The first board of deacons consisted of the following named Robert Williams, Elijah Bird, Dan Nelson, Milton Griffin and Berry Hickman

Rev Watts remained pastor of this church for about 20 years, during which time he baptized something like two thousand communicants

Present pastor Rev H B Southern Located corner Dowling and Lamar

WESLEY CHAPEL A M E CHURCH

To know, completely understand and appreciate one s church we must see what really was, know something of its origin, and its relation to the people The pioneers of Wesley held their first services in an old rope factory across the street from McIlhenny But, determined on serving God under their own vine and fig tree, they set about to organize and build a church The organization was perfected about forty years ago under the presiding eldership of Rev H Wilhite, and had as its first pastor Rev A G Moment The first building was erected in 1876 Moment was succeeded by Rev J R Bivan in 1877, who pastored the church for two years He was succeeded by C W Porter, Porter by J Harvey Jones and a long list of others, namely, Rev Randolph Willard, C A Harris, J P Howard and Warnach

The first persons to identify themselves as members of Wesley Chapel were Lucy Ann Waofl, Annie Sweeney, Emma Binks, Maranda Brown Sister Smallwood, Lucretia

Davis, Brother Henry Carvin Randolph returned to fill the unexpired term of Rev Willard It is remarkable in those dark days how the members and ministers of the church worked to preserve the church and make it grow, and the results of the unselfish efforts are still manifest in our present Wesley Lucretia Davis, then in public schools of Houston, first organized a Sunday School near McIlhenny and McKinney Rev Brown, who was then pastor of Brown's Chapel, was sent for to come and look at the new Sunday School During the visit of Bishop Ward to the city Rev Wilhite named the church Wesley and then the Sunday School that had been organized by Lucretia Davis was moved to the little frame building The Sunday School work so well begun by Mrs Davis was succeeded by Emma Lewis now Emma Banks The church was recruited from all ranks of society, from the lower as well as the higher To this, above all, it owes its greatness and success. A glance at the history and progress of the church is enough to make us know that somebody has worked mightily Coming behind the founders of the church were a number of young men possessed of vision and vigor, and into the veins of the church they poured rich blood The most distinguished among them were Rev J W Rankins, M D Moody, D J Hull, P C Hunt W H Young and A Gardan These names form a background from which we may easily determine the present rank and position of the church in the A M E connection In 1908 Rev W D Miller came to the church, and through his experience and influence and power the church, already great, took on new strength and growth, and Rev E J Howard in 1914 found there a membership of more than 800 and the church progressively organized in all of its branches

And now, with Rev Howard as pastor, having so wonderfully succeeded at other places, we are hoping to see even greater things Already, in less than a year, a large sum has been paid on the mortgage debt, and plans are now being put into execution for repairing the church, which is needed Out of respect to the founders and love for Wesley Chapel we will do whatsoever our hands find to do to make it foremost in the connection

THE CHURCH OF THE LIVING GOD
THE PILLAR AND GROUND OF THE TRUTH 1st TIM 3 15

Temple No 1—Located on the corner of Sherman and Saulnier Streets Elder James Pendleton, Pastor This local temple was organized by its present pastor in 1907, when without a single member or a five-cent piece, he pitched his camp on the Market House square There he preached and succeeded in gaining twenty members From there he located in the Second Ward, in the building now occupied as a church by Rev Wm Treadville

In the spring of 1908 the church purchased a 60x30-foot tent and moved to the Fourth Ward and leased from Major A Paul the vacant lot, corner Lyon and San Felipe Streets There we entered again upon the battle royal in the defense of the great Church of God, which He (God) purchased with His own blood Acts 20 28 And through many dangerous toils and snares, we succeeded in establishing a membership of 350

From there we moved into the Pan Hall above the E Jackson Undertaking Parlor, 1017 San Felipe Street, our membership steadily increasing It must be remembered that through these several years of no certain abiding place we were continually laving aside of our means for the vital moment, which came in the spring of 1909, when the church purchased for $600 00 the site of its present location And in 1911 we contracted for the present building that now adorns this beautiful site, being 50x30 feet clear floor space, with 30 feet hall in rear, built by our Deacon Board between their work hours

The present record shows a total membership of about 650, while these are not all active, there are some as good people in the church as the city affords The church house is equipped with all modern and sanitary conveniences and has among its auxiliaries the Woman's Charity Work, Sister C Spivey, President, Sister L Flowers, Vice-President, Sister L B Pendleton, Secretary A regular Sunday morning Bible Class, F R Griffin, teacher, A Fenel, Supt , a regular singing choir, Sister E Stafford, leader, Sister S Johnson, Secretary, a Ministers' and Deacons' Bible Extension Club, Elder C J Laws, President, A Fenel, Secretary, a board of six deacons, G W White, Chairman, A Pearson A Fenel, D Fisher L Robinson, S Montgomery, J W Hilton, Secretary

The church is now clear of debt except $75 00 on sanitation The religious morals of the Church of God have been and are to raise men and women from a dead level to a perpendicular and to diffuse such scriptural knowledge as will cause them to search the scriptures as commanded by Jesus Christ St John 5 39   J W HILTON, C C

1. Mr. and Mrs. Henry Franklin   4. Will Robinson   7. Mrs. E. C. Robinson   10. Dan A. Goodwin   13. Mrs. D. L. Jones
2. Sonnie Mason   5. Mrs. D. P. Holly   8. P. H. Watkins   11. Miss Sonnie Mason   14. Wm. McKinley Henry
3. Mrs. P. H. Watkins   6. T. C. Davenport   9. Miss Louise M. Brown   12. A. T. Bland   15. Mrs. M. E. Williams

REV. I. M. BURGAN, D. D.

A native of North Carolina, born 1848, Rev. Dr. Burgan received his education in the public schools and State Normal of Indiana and at Wilberforce University, Ohio, graduating from the university in the class of 1883. He became a communicant of the A. M. E. Church in 1870 and was married to Miss Cora M. Moore of Detroit, Mich., who was at the time teacher of music in the Blind Asylum at Austin, Texas, in 1889.

He came to Texas in 1883 to take charge of the Paul Quinn College as its president, which position he has held almost continually until 1914. During his nineteen years as president of the Paul Quinn College at Waco, he on two different times resigned, but the Board of Directors, feeling the need of his strong hand to guide the work, re-elected him. He is rated as one of the strongest educators of his race, and during his administration as president he had the distinction of graduating the first class with degrees ever graduated from a college of his race in the State.

Dr. Burgan has been quite prominent in all advance movements for his race. He has demonstrated his business capacity in the economic and almost wonderful management of Paul Quinn College during the "long, hard, lean years." He is a good preacher and stands in the front ranks of advance thinkers and active workers of his race. In his work and dealings he has enjoyed the fullest confidence of the leading people of both races. Some of the leading men of the white race of Waco voluntarily asked him to receive a recommendation from them attesting the esteem and confidence they had for and in him.

He began his ministerial career in 1887 and accepted his first pastorate in 1881. During his ministerial work he has pastored churches in Ohio, Indiana, California, Arkansas and Texas, with a marked degree of success. It is to men of this character and calibre that the masses of the race must look for their greatest human exemplars.

Paul Quinn College, Waco, Texas.

PAUL QUINN COLLEGE.

Above is a birdseye view of the Paul Quinn College of the A. M. E. Church, located at Waco, Texas, established in 1881 during the administration of Bishop R. H. Cain. This school occupies a campus of twenty acres, a good part of which is given over to farm demonstration work and the growing of vegetables, the sale of which has helped materially to finance the college. The United States Demonstration Farm Department has a sub-station on the campus. The group of buildings consist of twelve separate units. Even with these buildings, they are inadequate to take care of the patronage that would come to the college if larger accommodations were provided. The largest year the college has had since the organization noticed an attendance of 330 students. It is estimated that if more commodious buildings were provided this attendance would range from 500 to 700 annually. The faculty is composed of fifteen educators, headed by J. K. Williams, A. M., President, and J. H. Talton, B. S., Secretary. The degrees given are A. E., B. S. and B. D., the curriculum being on a par with similar college institutes, also includes agricultural and industrial training. Several of the agricultural exhibits have taken first prize at fairs, and the printing department took second prize at Dallas. A department of Carpentry is successfully operated.

Much of the progress of the school is attributed by the A. M. E. Church people and others to the able management of Dr. I. M. Burgan, who took the presidency of the college the third year of its existence. Bishop Smith succeeded during this last year in raising and liquidating a large mortgaged indebtedness which had hung over the property for about thirty years. The property is now worth $125,000.00.

This school has furnished the Afro-American race with many of its best teachers and has furnished the church to which it belongs with many of its strongest preachers and most active pastors, as well as giving to the race many prominent men in all professional callings. Despite the fact that on an average the church to which the college belongs is a comparatively poor one and the college has had a fierce struggle for advancement and a real struggle for life itself, it is regarded as one of the most successful colleges of the Southwest. The college is regarded by the best people of Waco and wherever it is known as a potent factor in the uplift of the race.

THE FULLNESS OF TIME

The Great Jehovah, in the "Fullness of Time,"
When all was chaos, without reason or rhyme,
Touched the world with finger sublime,
    And breathed in us the breath of life

Within each one a spirit was born,
A beauty, this cold, dumb clay to adorn,
And the world of darkness and death was shorn,
    And the pulse of each was rife

With thoughts of beauty and things divine,
With the light of Love in each heart to shine,
And all was mine and all was thine,
    Till dread Sin with its hydra head

Came into our midst with noisome tread
And brought to our hearts a mortal dread
And broken then was the golden thread
    That bound us to eternal life

Since then in the "Fullness of Time" again,
Jehovah in the form of lowly man,
Came to repair the broken strand
    That was cut by Sin's dread knife

And now each one in his lowly way,
Tho, still, helpless bound in lifeless clay
Can look forward to the glorious day
    When Eden shall come once more

No matter the race or tribe or skin,
The Master has said "Ye shall enter in."
And we are brothers and all are kin,
    Each bound for the other shore

Each belongs to the brotherhood of man,
The Fatherhood of God all tribes shall span
For this is Jehovah's cherished plan,
    And we are a part of Him

Part and parcel of things sublime,
And in the "Fullness" again of "Time,"
All will be Love and reason and rhyme,
    With Japhet and Ham and Shem

J. B. Bell's Residence, 2121 German Street.

Biography of J. B. BELL, Capitalist

On Christmas Day, 1858, there was born in Macon, Georgia, a child, under auspices almost as humble as were those of that other babe in Bethlehem of Judea, of whom we have it,—

"And this shall be a sign unto you; ye shall find a babe wrapped in swaddling clothes, lying in a manger."

Auspices almost as humble, for his parents had not the blessing of human liberty. But brilliant promise and a long life of usefulness were as an unseen halo around this young Negro boy's head and a fond mother named him John Brown, in gratitude to one who had risked all for a down-trodden race. She named him this, little knowing that it was prophetic of her child's future prominence as a civilian and of his public-spiritedness as a Christian gentleman.

BORN IN SLAVERY.

At the early age of six months his mother and father were torn asunder by the heart-breaking code of human slavery. The mother was brought with her children to Galveston, Texas, July, 1859. Immediately she was sold to Thomas Woods of Moscow, Polk County, Texas, at which place she was emancipated when her son, John Brown, reached the age of seven years. The third year thereafter his mother moved to Houston, where she died June 10, 1868, and was buried here. The young orphaned boy was cared for by a brother, Horace Bell, who died some years since.

HIS EDUCATION.

> "Books in the running brooks,
> Sermons in stones—And good in everything."

That it is true that all education is not found in books, is proven in the life of J. B. Bell, for he learned life's hardest lessons, not from the library or the university, but from stern contact with adversity. His school training covered the short period of three years and six months. The three years were spent in the public schools of Houston, Texas. At that point he had to go to work for himself. Much later, in his young manhood, he attended night school in Calvert, Texas, for three months, and when the teacher resigned, had so well qualified himself for the position that he was unanimously selected by the other students as teacher. In October of that year he entered Tillotson College, Austin, Texas, and remained there for three months, until the Christmas holidays.

HIS BUSINESS TRAINING.

He received his business training with the firm of Bell & Thornton, which firm conducted a grocery store in the Fifth Ward of Houston, Texas. This firm dissolved partnership in 1875 and the ambitious young boy was thrown out of employment at the age of thirteen years. Ambitious to support himself, he secured a position to attend the horse and buggy of Dr G A McDonell, of Houston Texas, which position he held for three years, 1875 to 1878, at a wage of $5 00 per month

September 15th, 1878, he left this position and went to Calvert, Texas, and was employed by his half-brother, L W Woods in the grocery and restaurant business He left this position to teach school in Robertson County, 1879 to 1881 It was in October of that year that he entered Tillotson College, and returned to Calvert to spend the Christmas holidays He left Calvert on the night of December 31st and arrived in Houston January 1st, 1882 He entered the employment of Reuben Thornton, grocer, for a wage of $30 00 per month and his board He remained here one year and one day, when Mr Thornton died, January 2, 1883 On January 15th, 1883, Mr Bell bought the business of Mrs Thornton for $315 00 This business he conducted for thirteen years and nine months and sold it out to L W Woods, April, 1896 At that time he entered fully into the real estate business on his own account At this time he had a rental income of $216 00 a month By patience, thrift and business foresight he has increased his business to a present rental income of over $600 00 a month

HIS MARRIAGE TO MISS ALLEN

In 1896 he began courting Miss Venora Allen, daughter of the Honorable Richard Allen, and they were happily married July, 1900 Before the marriage he had erected a modern residence of seven rooms, and it was in readiness to welcome his bride Since that time he has increased the home to one of ten rooms

It is a palatial residence, richly furnished front and back stairways, double parlors opening into a spacious entrance hall and continuing the reception suite into the library and dining room The sleeping apartments are upstairs, built along lines of Southern architecture, with sweeping verandas about The home is valued at $5,000 00

Mrs Bell is a sweet and gracious matron, who rejoices in extending hospitality to her numerous friends Handsome, winning in disposition, affable and pleasant, she is a hostess whose invitations are received with pleasure and every recipient thereof is assured of a welcome, hearty and sincere

SOCIETY CONNECTIONS

In 1885 Mr Bell was elected Master of Solomon Lodge of the United Brothers of Friendship, and served in this capacity twenty-five years During that time the body bought one-half interest in a three-story hall at a cost of over $5,000 00 He has attended many sessions of the Grand Lodge of U B of F's, and has represented his local order there He is now a member of the Board of Commissioners of the Grand Lodge of U B of F's of the State of Texas along with four other estimable gentlemen, viz W F Bledsoe, Grand Master, F W Gross, Grand Secretary, Joe Nichols, Grand Treasurer, N E Jones (of Gonzales), J B Bell

At his recommendation two brick buildings on Milam Street, within one-half block of the City Market, were purchased by the U B of F s at a cost of $150,000 00 He yet helps to supervise the rentals of that property and its maintenance

He has been elected twice as Chancellor Commander of True Friends Lodge, Knights of Pythias of the City of Houston, and has often represented his local order in Grand Lodge Mr Bell is also a member of the Masonic Magnolia Lodge No 2

NATIONAL NEGRO BUSINESS LEAGUE

In 1906, in company with the Reverend Jno Covington of Houston, Texas, Mr Bell visited the National Negro Business League at Atlanta, Georgia The following year he attended the session of the same League at Topeka Kansas He addressed the gathering in a pleasing and forceful manner on the subject of Real Estate and Loans So profoundly impressed were his auditors that they hailed his address with thunderous applause, and at that sitting elected Mr Bell as a member of the executive committee of the National Negro Business League, of which Mr Booker T Washington, the sage of Tuskegee, is president He is still a member of that body and has attended all of its sessions since that date

In January of 1910 the executive committee met in the City of New York and while there they were guests in the home of Mr Andrew Carnegie, philanthropist, for two hours

HIS PUBLIC-SPIRITEDNESS

A few years ago Mr Emmett J Scott wrote Rev W H Logan that Houston could get a public library for colored citizens Several meetings were held and, among others, Mr Bell was interested Committees were formed and sent to visit Mayor Rice of the City of Houston, and seemingly the committee made no headway Mr T H Fairchild requested J B Bell to go and see the Mayor as he knew him personally He went and requested Mayor Rice to make an appropriation of $1,500 00 a year to maintain the Library, since Mr Carnegie's requirements for establishing such an institution in a given city were that the said city should furnish the sum of $1,500 00 yearly for the upkeep of the Library Mayor Rice requested that they buy the ground first

When this was reported to the citizens in a meeting, J B Bell was made chairman of the purchasing committee He went to St James Lodge No 6, of which W E Jones was the Worthy Master, and coupled with his aid, he purchased a lot on the corner of Frederick and Robin Streets, Fourth Ward, at a cost of $1,500 00 The committee had only $500 00 on hand at that time and Mr Bell offered to loan them $1,000 00 They accepted the loan and the lot was purchased of the Lodge for that amount, and he afterward, with others, helped to solicit the money to repay the loan After the deed was received from the Lodge, he visited Mayor Rice and showed the deed and immediately the appropriation of $1,500 00 yearly was made That being completed, he took up correspondence with W Sidney Pittman of Washington, D C, to draw the plans and specifications for the building at a cost of $750 00 for the plans and superintendence of the construction, with Mr Bell as assistant superintendent, until completion of the building

A Board of Trustees of which he is a member, was formed, and he was also elected as business manager.

This prominent corner was secured for the location of the Library and soon a modern structure was reared "to help turn the darkness into day" for the Negro It stands, a beautiful home of culture, of concrete and brick, ornamental, well-designed, with well-kept grass plots, shrubbery, flowers and baskets of fern,—

"Learning's pleasant seat."—

a source of pride to the Negro population of Houston and a credit to any people It furnishes employment to a Librarian, an Assistant Librarian and a Janitor

Mr Bell was also elected Treasurer of this Board, which position he has held continuously from the beginning He makes a monthly report to the Mayor of Houston and also a yearly report of finances which amount to $1,500 00 a year

For fourteen years Mr Bell was a member of the Board of Trustees and Treasurer of Emancipation Park Association He has served once as Secretary and once as President during that term of years W E Jones was President of the Board at that time and all improvements that Emancipation Park has known were established during that time, the building of fences, two pavilions, restaurants and the construction of the race track

Several years after the ministration of that Board, a new Board was elected with H M Freeman as President They borrowed $3,000 00 from H Masterson of Houston, Texas, to be paid within three years, $1,000,00 a year with interest at 10 per cent The first note of the series, No 1, fell due on May 19, 1914, and the Board did not have the money to pay it They reported to Mr Bell that they had tried all over Houston to get some one to take it up and were unable to find anyone They came to him on the 18th of May Against the Emancipation Park at this time were two suits pending in the courts of Houston, and his attorney advised him not to make the loan He did so, however, over his objections, and readily consented to take up the note and thus saved the foreclosure on the land He said · "I would rather lose $1,000 00 than see my people lose their Park Since that time the Board has paid $1,000 00, without interest to Mr Bell, and he stands ready to pay the other $2 000 00, if by chance they can not meet the other notes on the date, rather than see the colored people lose their Park

The Colored Federated Charities, an organization which co-operates with the white organization of like nature and has for its purpose helping the unfortunate and poverty-stricken of our race, appointed a committee to see the County Commissioners Court and request an appropriation of $5,000 00 for the establishment of a Farm School for Delinquent Colored Youths The request was readily granted The following men served on that committee J B Bell, Sam Wilson, J J Hardeway, Nat Q Henderson Mr Bell holds the position also of Acting Vice President of the Association and the Hon Rufus Cage, President of the Houston School Board is President

The Judge of the County Commissioners Court, Hon W H Ward, suggested to the committee that they see the Mayor and request a similar appropriation They did so during the month of November, 1914, and on December 24, 1914, the Mayor, Hon Mr Ben H Campbell, said that he and the City Commissioners had concluded to join with the county and make another appropriation of $5,000 00 for Colored Delinquent Youths The Mayor assured Mr Bell that he would see the County Judge at once and make the purchase of the ground, one hundred acres for the school and all necessary improvements, and they felt that their persistent efforts had been greatly rewarded To say that their gratitude to the Mayor and City Commissioners the Judge and County Commissioners was great would be expressing it mildly A typewritten letter of appreciation was presented to each gentleman and a box of cigars with Christmas greetings along with it The following compose the gentlemen who united in passing on this kind of expression of their appreciation Mr J B Bell, Mr Nat Q Henderson, Mr Sam Wilson and Prof Jas D Ryan, and these are the city and county officials who were the recipients of the same City Commissioners of Houston—Messrs J J Pastoriza, H A Halverton, Dave Fitzgerald, Matt Drennan County Commissioners are Messrs V Barker, W H Lloyd W H Keiser, W A Smith An excerpt from the letter of appreciation is that —

"We take occasion to express our thanks and appreciation to you, individually and collectively, for your attitude in concluding to make an appropriation for the establishment of a Farm Training School for Delinquent Youths

"We assure you that our people appreciate most highly your efforts to ameliorate their condition in this particular, and we all note with pride your concern and interest in doing things which tend toward the progressiveness of our city, not omitting our own people, even "

J B BELL, Acting Vice-President
NAT Q HENDERSON Supt
JAS D RYAN, Secretary

Mr J B Bell was chairman of a movement for colored citizens, the parallel of which America has not known Prof J D Ryan, Nat Q Henderson, Sam Wilson and J B Bell worked as heroes in a movement that brought Christmas cheer to Houston s poor children, in that great, public building, the Auditorium, along with the hearty co-operation of such estimable gentlemen as Hon Ben H Campbell, Mavor of Houston, and Rev W S Lockhart No other city throws open the doors to its most splendid building to white and black alike and extends to the citizens equal charity, as does Houston Provisions and clothing for the poor were given The schools were interested and had collected many gifts for the unfortunate

The following resolutions were offered by the chairman, J B Bell

"Whereas, The City of Houston, through the instrumentality of Dr Lockhart and its Mayor, Hon Ben Campbell, acting through the City Council, has seen fit to furnish a Christmas tree to the colored citizens of the city, and

Whereas, This is the instance the like of which has not occurred within the United States of America, and

Whereas, It has granted the use of the spacious Auditorium for the occasion, and

Whereas, A large number of white citizens have in various ways contributed to the success of the movement, be it

Resolved, That we do by a vote of thanks express our sincere appreciation to the City of Houston, to Dr Lockhart and all who in the spirit of Christ, Whose birthday we celebrate, have in any way by word or deed assisted in this great unprecedented and unparalleled manifestation of charity

J B BELL, Chairman
J J GILMORE
NAT Q HENDERSON
W J SMITH
E O SMITH "

Mr Bell is a deacon of Antioch Baptist Church and has been Treasurer of same church for several years

He is the owner of a large seven-passenger Cadillac, the cut of which appears in these pages, and he and his wife are generous dispensers of their hospitality with the same They purchased a large car so as to be able to carry their friends along with them on their pleasure jaunts and across-country tours A noted instance of their generosity with their automobile is proven in the fact that they have on several occasions, loaned it to the family of Dr G A McDonell, a white gentleman, now in modest circumstances, but one to whom Mr Bell feels that he owes a great deal for his start in life, having once been in his employment

Mr Bell is a modest, unassuming man, who goes about among his fellows, smiling and cheerful, upright and fearless, king over his word, with no tinge of hauteur in his makeup, humble as the least of them

Thanking God for his blessings, trusting in Him for the future, he shares his blessings with his fellowmen He possesses that rare gift that well becomes any man, in any station of life, the pleasing trait of remembering faces well One man said of him recently "He is one of nature's noblemen He is a citizen who meets the most humble in that cordial manner which says 'Truly, I am glad to meet you "

COL. WILLIAM WYNDON.

Colonel Wm. Wyndon. Cabinet-maker; 1620 Pannell. Born in Shreveport, La., in 1868; attended Straties University of New Orleans one year. Came to Houston in 1894. Married Miss Helen Garland in 1894. Professed religion in 1880 and joined Sloan Memorial M. E. Church in 1895. Was made an Odd Fellow in 1896; Knight of Pythias in 1907; U. B. of F. in 1908; A. F. & A. M. in 1912; Pilgrim in 1910. At present holding offices in the following orders: Lieut. Col. in command of the Ninth Patriarch Regiment of Texas G. U. O. O. F.; Major of the Second Battalion, First Regiment of Texas K. of P.; Knight Commander of the Knights of Friendship of the Jurisdiction of Texas, U. B. of F. Locally: P. S. of Summer Lodge No. 1021, G. U. O. O. F.; K. of R. and S., Washington Lodge No. 88, K. of P.; W. S. of South Gate Lodge No. 195, U. B. of F.; Worthy Shepherd of Myrtle Spray Sanctuary No. 281, A. O. of P.; Grand Secretary of Past Grand Masters Council No. 75, G. U. O. O. F.; Worthy Patriarch Recorder of Houston Patriarch No. 159, G. U. O. O. F.

High School Corner San Felipe and Frederick Streets.

Paul Lawrence Dunbar School, Glass and Liberty Streets.

Douglass School, corner McGowen and Palke Sts.

Luckie School, corner Palmer and Lamar Sts.

Gregory School, 1303 Wilson Street.

Booker T. Washington School, corner Bingham and Colorado Sts.

Manual Training Department, Frederick St

Frederick Douglass School, 2302 Center Street

Longston School, 2309 German Street

B. K. Bruce School, 1705 Robinson Street

Harrisburg School.

Mrs. S. G. Kay, Principal.

Harris County School Teachers.

1. Mrs. Rhoda Kay
2. Mrs. Van H. McKinney
3. Miss Pearl Parker
4. Miss Helen Bright
5. Miss Ruby Sholars
6. Miss Mazie J. Spencer
7. Mrs. Maud L. Palmer
8. Miss Lattie Alford
9. Mrs. Rosa Lee Foster

10. Miss Ida L. Green
11. Mrs. Olivia Mitchell
12. Mrs. S. G. Kay
13. Mrs. Ardalia Boone
14. Mrs. N. E. Jackson
15. Miss Eugenia Cobb
16. Miss Georgia Buckner
17. Mrs. Milton Griffin
18. Mr. Fisher Barnes

19. Mrs. V. A. DeWalt
20. Miss Natalie Green
21. Miss Mamie Curry
22. Mrs. I. M. Mitchell
23. Miss O. A. Mason
24. Mr. Geo. B. Sanders
25. Mr. Herbert Mitchell
26. Mr. C. C. Tate

27. Mr. L. W. Haynes
28. Miss Annie Dixon
29. Miss Annie Verrette
30. Miss Nancy Cook
31. Mr. O. L. Hubbard
32. Miss Vernella Farris
33. Mr. J. T. Thompson
34. Miss Aurelia Rucker

SCHOOLS AND TEACHERS

HIGH SCHOOL—CORNER SAN FELIPE AND FREDERICK.

NAME.	POSITION.	ADDRESS.
Jas. D. Ryan	Principal	2007 Hamilton
P. H. Holden	History	2917 Turner
A. V. Strickland	Algebra	215 Robin
V. B. Miller	Latin	217 Robin
Viola Webber	English	319 Robin
W. L. D. Johnson	Science	2415 Dowling
E. D. Pierson	Seventh Grade	318 Robin
R. G. Lockett	High Sixth Grade	2613 Nance
G. E. Morrow	Low Sixth Grade	215 Robin
Mary J. Holden	Domestic Science	2917 Turner
R. M. Catchings	Manual Training	2618 Rice
J. H. Rievas	Mechanical Drawing	2003 Live Oak
Cecelia Scott	Domestic Science	2721 Opelousas
Theresa Matthews	Supernumerary	912 Lamb

FRED DOUGLASS SCHOOL—CORNER McGOWEN AND LIVE OAK.

NAME.	POSITION.	ADDRESS.
W. S. Francis	Principal	1815 Jackson
C. F. Smith	Arithmetic	3201 Center
Rachael Pendleton	English	2402 St. Charles
Daisy Crafton	History and Geography	2301 McGowan
La Bertha Perry	Reading	1212 Robin
Mac E. Smith	Fourth Grade	2302 St. Charles
Florida Williams	Third Grade	1314 Railroad
Maggie Hearne	Third Grade	2320 Dowling
Mabel Oler	Low Third Grade	3602 Preston
Melissa Price	Low Third Grade	2319 Dowling
Lucile Bryant	Low Third Grade	219 Stratford
Della M. Booker	Second Grade	2116 Dowling
Trula Jones	Second Grade	1204 Andrews
Lucy Booker	High First Grade	2116 Dowling
Annie M. White	First Grade	1614 Sherman
M. B. Everett	First Grade	611 Calhoun
Edna Millard	Supernumerary	108 Denver
P. Williams	Supernumerary	1715 Ennis

GREGORY SCHOOL—CORNER CLEVELAND AND WILSON.

NAME.	POSITION.	ADDRESS.
W. E. Miller	Principal	310 Robin
S. B. Williams	Low Fifth Grade	1412 Cleveland
Simonetta Criner	High Fourth Grade	913 Cleveland

GREGORY SCHOOL—Continued

NAME	POSITION	ADDRESS
Lillian Clark	Low Fourth Grade	1416 Grove
Fannie Alexander	High Third Grade	1218 Wilson
Nellie Johnson	Low Third Grade	618 Robin
Mary McCarter	Second Grade	1712 Houston Ave
Willie Blount	High Second Grade	611 Robin
Wessie Grimes	Low Second Grade	2419 Chenevert
Bessie A Neal	First Grade	1720 Edwards
Euretta Fairchild	High First Grade	2019 Dallas
Alice Johnson	Low First Grade	2415 Dowling
Ada B Price	Low First Grade	1102 West
Edna Banks		3110 St Charles
Mamie Robinson	Supernumerary	519 Robin

PAUL L DUNBAR SCHOOL—CORNER CLARK AND LIBERTY.

NAME	POSITION	ADDRESS
B H Grimes	Principal	2419 Chenevert
B H Watson	Sixth Grade	1018 Fuller
Dora Johnson	High Fourth and Low Fifth	3004 Live Oak
Tommie Lee	Fourth Grade	1503 Maury
Penny Collins	High Third Grade	909 St Charles
Ollie Phillips	Low Third Grade	2303 McGowen
Pearle Parker	High Second Grade	1205 Robin
Bertha Crawford	Low Second Grade	99 Hill
Vincy Keys	First Grade	1315½ Congress
Emma J Jones	First Grade	2020 St Emanuel
Maud Connor	Low First Grade	1018 Hill
Selma Perry	Supernumerary	1212 Robin
Rebecca Ransom	Supernumerary	

BOOKER T WASHINGTON SCHOOL—BINGHAM AND COLORADO

NAME	POSITION	ADDRESS
E O Smith	Principal	1214 O'Neil
Reva Green	Fifth Grade	1910 La Branch
E S Kennard	Fourth Grade	1009 Robin
Minnie Milligan	Third Grade	1205 Andrew
Bessie Love	Second Grade	906 Andrew
Narcissa Hill	First Grade	407 San Felipe
Mamie Robey	Supernumerary	1509 La Branch

LANGSTON GRADE SCHOOL—GERMAN STREET

NAME	POSITION	ADDRESS
W J Smith	Principal	1310 Sherman
V P Waiters	Sixth Grade	3012 Polk
Etta O'Neill	Fifth Grade	--
D E Miller	Fourth Grade	1712 Smith
Earlie Lawrence	Third Grade	2102 Dowling
Ellouise Matthews	Third Grade	3442 Dennis

LANGSTON GRADE SCHOOL—Continued

NAME	POSITION	ADDRESS
W B Anderson	Second Grade	2912 Liberty
Ivor Webb	First Grade	2109 Liberty
Cadie S Wilson	First Grade	2103 Rusk
Laura E Payne	Domestic Science	2106 Jefferson
Lois Fortson	Supernumerary	

LUCKIE GRADE SCHOOL—LAMAR AND RICE STREETS

NAME	POSITION	ADDRESS
J N Dodson	Principal	1305 Andrews
A W H Lee	Sixth Grade	2901 Shepherd
W E Brandon	Low Fifth Grade	307½ San Felipe
Mable Fairchild	Low Fourth Grade	2019 Dallas
Josephine Taylor	Third Grade	2410 Dallas
Sallie Hogan	Third Grade	2215 Tuam
Lydia Hawkins	Second Grade	1407 Cook
Mary J Tolbert	Low First Grade	2712 Capitol
Jno Blount	Manual Training	1710 Live Oak
Willie Belle Parker	Supernumerary	910 Robin

B K BRUCE SCHOOL—BREMOND AND CONTI STREETS

NAME	POSITION	ADDRESS
Nat Q Henderson	Principal	3019 Nance
J C Sanderson	Third Grade.	3004 Live Oak
Uxenia Scott	Third Grade	2721 Opelousas
Celia Scott	Second Grade	2721 Opelousas
Sallie May	First Grade	2303 Freeman
Cora Conway	Supernumerary	1601 Jackson

FRANCIS HARPER SCHOOL—CHANEYVILLE

NAME	POSITION	ADDRESS
G B M Turner	Principal	1307 Andrew
Hattie Prevost	Third Grade	1303 Andrew
Jewell Taylor		2604 McKinney
Rosa Watson	First and Second Grades	1018 Fuller
Illma Lawrence	Supernumerary	2101 Dowling

HOLLYWOOD SCHOOL—WASHINGTON AVENUE

NAME	POSITION	ADDRESS
Mable Wesley	First and Second Grades	1014 Hill
Adine J Scott	First Grade	1014 Hill

GLEN COVE SCHOOL—SCOTT STREET

NAME	POSITION	ADDRESS
J H Berry	Principal	
Samie O King	First and Second Grades	1415 Saulnier

GREEN POND SCHOOL—SAN FELIPE ROAD

NAME	POSITION	ADDRESS
Maggie Chester	Teacher	910 Hemer

BRAY'S BAYOU SCHOOL—ALMEDA ROAD

NAME	POSITION	ADDRESS
Mrs Adele B Jones	Teacher	

M H BROYLES

M H Broyles was born in Anderson County, South Carolina, November 10, 1863, the eleventh of eighteen children born of the union of Robert and Malinda Broyles

In childhood he attended the public schools of his native county, entered Claflin University, South Carolina Agricultural College and Mechanics' Institute in the fall of 1882, from which institution he was graduated with honors on May 23, 1888

In the summer of 1888 he came to Texas, adopting the Lone Star State as his future home, taught a county school in McLennan County during the winter of 1888-89, having distinguished himself as a ripe and thorough scholar in his first examination at Waco, Texas, in October, 1888 During the summer of 1889 he taught Mathematics in the Waco Summer Normal Institute, was elected Secretary of the Colored Men's Convention of Texas, and after winning in competitive examination, was elected to the principalship of the Brenham High School for the term of 1889-90

In June, 1890, he was elected to the associate principalship of the Prairie View State Normal and Industrial College of Texas, resigning the position three years later to accept the principalship of the Hearne Academy Normal and Industrial Institute, which position he resigned in 1896 to accept the chair of Mathematics in the Prairie View State Normal and Industrial College of Texas, filling the same until 1904, when he left the profession of teaching to make preparation to enter the practice of the law, being admitted to the Texas Bar on August 12, 1905, and to the United States District and Circuit Courts on March 8, 1906, and has since practiced law in Houston, Texas, where he enjoys the confidence of the bench and bar

In 1891 he represented the State of Texas as one of the delegates to the International Educational Association at Toronto, Canada, was elected President of the Colored State Teachers' Association of Texas in 1895, conducted the State School of Methods at Houston, Texas, in 1899, organized the Texas Negro Convention of Texas in 1902, and organized and established the Orgen Realty & Investment Company in 1903

Was on the delegation from the State at large to the National Republican Convention at Chicago in 1912, and was the Republican nominee for the State Legislature of Texas from Harris County in 1914 Established and published the Texas Independent from 1894 to 1896

On the 10th day of August, A D 1897, he was united in marriage with Miss Mary J Moore, the sole surviving daughter of A L Moore of Austin, Texas, and of this union eight (8) children have been born, to-wit Theresa Ruth, Grace Beatrice, Mary Hannetta, Theodore Frederick (who died in infancy), Portia Louise, Robbie Lee, Major Hannon, Jr, and Agnes Valeria

In religion Mr Broyles is a Baptist, never having formally severed his connection with his mother church—Mount Zion Baptist Church of Belton, South Carolina

M. H. Broyles and Family and Residence, San Felipe Road.

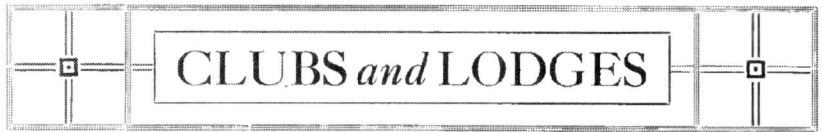

CLUBS and LODGES

ANCIENT ORDER OF PILGRIMS.

Victoria. No. 1; Hearts of Oak, No. 2; Hardy, No. 4; Rose of Sharon, No. 12; Lily of the Valley, No. 13; Golden Rule, No. 16; Faithful Laborers, No. 34; Golden Sceptre, No. 36; Earnest Workers, No. 37; Olive Leaf, No. 39; Pride of Houston, No. 109; Star of East, No. 172; Silver Circle, No. 177; Olive Branch, No. 203; Prosperous, No. 210; Phoenix, No. 213; Morning Glory, No. 223; Saint Carmac, Houston Heights. No. 228; Chancyville Pride. No. 235; Earnest Seekers, No. 240; Joel, Brunner, No. 246; Taft. No. 263; Sunshine, No. 264; True Friends, No. 273; Nimrod, No. 274; Pride of Antioch, No. 277; Myrtle Spray, No. 281; Theola, No. 301; Hiram, No. 303; Dunbar, No. 304; Independent, No. 311.

GRAND UNITED ORDER OF ODD FELLOWS.

The G. U. O. of O. F. was organized in Houston in 1881, August 16th, making Odd Fellowship 34 years old. At that time it was very small, but since then it has grown very strong financially and numerically. There are several local bodies. The men's department numbers about 600, the women's department about the same. The Odd Fellows own a very nice hall and rent house which is valued at about $5,000. The hall is located at the corner of Crosby and Hobson Streets. Their regular anniversary is August 16th. Their annual Thanksgiving is the second Sunday in May of each year. The G. U. O. of O. F. has two classes of policies, $300.00 and $500.00, also they give a $75.00 funeral outside of the policies. The G. U. O. of O. F., Council No. 75, in Houston.

United Sons of Liberty Lodge, No. 1946; Golden Shield Lodge, No. 2082; Summer Lodge, No. 4021; Golden Rule Lodge, No. 6392; Damascus Lodge, No. 7188; Silver Rock Lodge, No. 7773; Gold Spar Lodge, No. 7775; Light of Houston Lodge, No. 7776; Roberta Lodge, Houston Heights, No. 7952; Paul Dunbar Lodge, No. 9394.

KNIGHTS AND DAUGHTERS OF TABOR.

Earnest Workers' Temple, No. 12; Good Will Temple, No. 27; Smith Temple, No. 50; E. M. Fisher Temple, No. 105; C. E. W. Day Temple, No. 130; St. Clair Temple, No. 145; Bright Light Temple, No. 249; Mt. Ararat Temple, No. 295; Heights Temple, No. 363; Brunner Temple, No. 373; Moses Temple, No. 393; Dunbar Temple, No. 514.

KNIGHTS AND DAUGHTERS OF TABOR.

Golden Gate Tabernacle, No. 28; Elector Tabernacle, No. 30; True Daughters Tabernacle, No. 45; Marechal Neil Rose Tabernacle, No. 50; Queen Esther Tabernacle, No. 59; Earnest Workers Tabernacle, No. 78; Reedy Tabernacle, No. 82; Sarah Hazel Tabernacle, No. 89; S. E. Johnson Tabernacle, No. 112, Prince Albert Rose Tabernacle, No. 135; Mittie Anna Tabernacle, No. 170; Golden Day Tabernacle, No. 174; Willing Workers Tabernacle, No. 175; Queen of the South Tabernacle, No. 186; True Friend Tabernacle,

No 230, Lone Star Tabernacle, No 259, Alpha Tabernacle, No 276, Sarah Haskell Tabernacle, No 368, Industrial Tabernacle, No 379, Metropolitan Tabernacle, No 456, Rubie's Pride Tabernacle, No 455, Oreo Leaf Tabernacle, No 474, Lowe's Faithful Tabernacle, No 529, Royal Tabernacle, No 553, American Beauty Tabernacle, No 579, Queen Daughters Tabernacle, No 630, Magdalene Tabernacle, No 778, Progress Tabernacle, No 794, Francis Ford Tabernacle, No ——

KNIGHTS AND DAUGHTERS OF TABOR

Silver Leaf Tent, No 4; True Love Tent, No 206 Ford's Tent, No 212, Calvin's Tent, No 316

KNIGHTS OF PYTHIAS

Sheet Anchor Lodge, No 19, Gold Spur Lodge, No 62, Washington Lodge, No 88, True Friend Iodge, No 119, Pythian Pride Lodge No 135, Golden Eagle Lodge, No 181 Harrisburg, Pride of Houston Lodge No 211, Pythagorian Lodge, No 267, Bright Star Lodge, No 283, Mt Olive Lodge. No 303, Stark's Memorial Lodge, No 411

KNIGHTS OF PYTHIAS (COURTS)

Hernyson Court, No 4, Dixon Court, No 46, Stellida Pride Court, No 80, Markham Rose Court, No 134, Zenith Court, No 221, Timberlake Court, No 260

MASONIC LODGES OF HOUSTON

Magnolia Lodge, No 3 Silver Trowel Lodge, No 47, Maple Leaf Lodge, No 147, Smithsonian Lodge, No 155, True Level Lodge, No 226, Heights Lodge, No 280, City of Refuge Lodge, No 287

HEROINES OF JERICHO

Mrs R A Winn, M A G M, Chapel Hill, Texas, Miss Annie B Isaacs, M A D G M, Bremond, Texas, Mrs N S Mosley, S G M, Fort Worth, Texas, Mrs A M Foster, J G M, Denison, Texas, Hon W M McDonald, W G J Fort Worth, Texas, Mrs R G McKinney, A G T, Sherman, Texas, Mrs A Z Hester, A G S, Houston, Texas, Mrs O V E Barlett, R G S, Prairie View, Texas

Mrs A Z Hester has been the former Grand Matron for five years after serving for four years as M G A she resigned to accept the office she now holds The H of J is noted throughout the length and breadth of this country for the many deeds of kindness to the suffering There are four local Courts in the City of Houston, as follows Hester Court, No 57, Valley of Eadon Court, No 84, Pearly Gate Court, No 98, and Corinthia Court, No 147

UNITED BROTHERS OF FRIENDSHIP

The United Brothers of Friendship was organized August 1, 1861, by Marshall W Taylor, W H Gipson, W N Hazelton Charles B Morgan, William Lawson, William Anderson, Wallace Jones and others of Louisville, Kentucky

The officers of the Texas Branch of United Brothers of Friendship are   Grand

Master, W F Bledsoe, Marshall, Deputy Grand Master, D A Starks, Hempstead, Grand Secretary, F W Gross, Houston, Grand Treasurer, Joseph Nichols, Houston

Up to the first day of January, 1915, it had collected for widows and orphans $712 347 60, and for other purposes $250 000 00 Office building on the corner of Prairie and Milam Streets, Houston, Texas, is worth $200,000 00   Our annual receipts are $150,000 00

The bonds mortgage notes and other investments amount to $35,000 00, and the proceeds from the rents and investments amount to $12 000 00 annually

UNITED BROTHERS OF FRIENDSHIP

St James Lodge, No 6, Solomon Lodge, No 18, Harrison Lodge, No 34, South Gate Lodge, No 195, Leonidas Lodge, No 203, Perrander Lodge, No 204, Selstin Lodge No 236 Foraker Lodge, No 248, Star of Houston Lodge, No 290, Men of Mark Lodge, No 310

SISTERS OF THE MYSTERIOUS TEN

Rebecca Temple, No 2, Goddess of Hope Temple, No 11, Earnest Workers Temple, No 37, Bethesda Temple, No 56, Lone Star Temple, No 57, Antioch Temple, No 197, Beautiful Queen Temple, No 203, Eastern Beauty Temple, No 207, Venus Temple, No 208, True Workers Temple, No 228, Houston Pride Temple, No 239 St Georgian Temple, No 240, Hollywood Temple, No 275, Rose Croix Temple, No 276, Concordia Temple, No 295.

Married Ladies' Social Club—Mrs H J Ewell, President, Mis L Allen, Vice-President   Meets once each month at the homes of the members for charity work

Magnolia Dramatic Club—Organized 1910   Object is to help church pay off debts and charity work P H McClough, President, R B H Yates, Manager, Mrs P H Harmon, Secretary

Married Ladies' Progressive Club—Meets at members' homes second and fourth Fridays Mrs F J Mitchell, President, Mrs Jennie Clark, Treasurer, Mrs L S Scott, Vice-President, Mis Annie McKinney, Secretary

Colored Woman's Fratricidal Club—Meets first Wednesday in each month at Social Rest Room, 409½ Milam Street Mrs M L Jones, President, Miss Hill, Vice-President, Mis A L Feagan, Secretary, Mis Mollie Washington, Assistant Secretary, Mis M E Miller, Treasurer

Hotel Men's Benevolent Association—Meets first and third Thursdays at 8 30 p m Odd Fellow Hall, corner Crosby and Hopson Streets H J Mitchell, President, Will Danniels, Vice-President Ed Jones, Secretary, Donaly Treasurer

Texas Negro Fair Association—Meets once each year at 714½ Prairie Avenue R H Hart, President; Jim Bulock, Vice-President, O M Miller, Treasurer, H J Mitchell, Chairman of Trustee Board

LOCAL ORDERS OF THE HOUSEHOLD OF RUTH, G U O O F

Household No   197—Mrs Dr B J Covington, W R, Dowling and Hadley
Household No   219—Mis E Sims, W R, 2303 Clay Avenue
Household No   1162—Mrs Katie Lewis, W R, 1614 Pannell Street
Household No   3015—Mrs Ella Daniel, W R, Harrisburg, Texas
Household No   4065—Mrs. 1 E Perry, W R, 1212 Robin
Household No   4236—Mrs Mollie Washington, W R, 1517 Colorado

Residence of Prof. W. E. Miller, 810 Robin Street.

Mrs. W. E. Miller.

Prof. W. E. Miller.

Miss Lillian E. Miller.

The Pierson Family.

Reading from left to right—E. D. Pierson, Jr., E. D. Pierson, Sr., Mrs. L. L. Pierson, Theodore D. Pierson and Eulalia V. Pierson

Nine years ago Prof. E. D. Pierson and family came here from Pittsburg, Texas, where he was principal of the City School, to head the Literary Department of Houston College. The interesting sketch below of his earlier as well as his later career is self-explanatory.

Mr. Edward Donahue Pierson, born of slave parentage, in the early 70's, joined the church of his mother's choice—Baptist—at the age of 15 years, and has been active in the religious, as well as the professional and business life of his people ever since.

Having an insatiable appetite for knowledge in general, he soon looked beyond the meager advantages offered in the poorly conducted public schools of his native State (Louisiana) and landed, poverty-hobbled, in Bishop College, Marshall, Texas, January, 1892. While at first the better-favored "city chaps" were wont to poke fun at this "raw" country boy, he soon became deservedly popular with both the student body and faculty—the president, N. Wolverton, a white Northern man, took especial interest in him, gave him an opportunity to "work his way" through school and one of his confidential men in college affairs.

It was during his college days, when he had not only to "work his way," but support a mother as well, that he learned the printer's trade and managed that department of the college along with other duties. He graduated from the professional course of Bishop College in 1895, and later returned and completed the college course in 1904, with the highest mark and honor of his class—receiving the degree of Bachelor of Science.

Recently Built Residence of Prof. E. D. Pierson, 318 Robin Street.

As a teacher, Mr. Pierson stands among the first. He is now teacher in the Colored High School of Houston, Secretary State B. Y. P. U. Convention, Treasurer of St. James Lodge U. B. F. (possibly the richest in Texas), President Houston Negro Business League, Deacon Antioch Baptist Church, Manager and Treasurer of the Western Star Publishing Co., the biggest all-around printing plant (colored) in Texas, and Managing Editor of the Western Star, a seven-column, 8-page weekly, the mouthpiece of Texas Negro Baptists.

Mr. Pierson is the happy father of three children Miss Eulalia Viola, who graduated head of her class from the Houston Colored High School; Theodore D., in high tenth grade, and Edward Donahue, Jr., in low eighth grade. "Everybody works and father," seems to be the slogan of this interesting family.

Unlike the average young man, Mr. Pierson seeks the hard and difficult things of life as stepping stones to the higher. If pluck, tact, square dealing and what not are elements of greatness, he should have a place among the great. Prof. Pierson, young and brilliant, fearless, yet congenial, is making for himself a record in the religious, business and literary world worthy a page in the history of any race.

Excerpt from "Who's Who Among the Colored Baptists."

Prof. P. H. Holden, B. S.   Mrs. P. H. Holden.

Mr. and Mrs. J. H. Harmon and J. H., Jr.

Prof. B. H. Grimes.

Residence of Prof. B. H. Grimes, 2419 Chenevert.

Prof. Grimes was born May 4, 1860, in Trinity County, Texas. He married Miss Bettie Arnett, December, 1878, and two children were the issue of this union. He came to Houston in 1887 and has since accumulated some very valuable property, some of which is in one of the best white districts of the city. He is a member of the M. E. Church and two fraternal societies, namely: The K. of P. and A. O. of P., the latter of which he served as Supreme Shepherd of Texas. He has been teaching twenty-nine years. It was while serving as janitor of the City High School in 1894 that he made the highest mark in a competitive teachers' examination, and was immediately assigned to work in the city schools as teacher. He exhibited so much natural ability as a teacher and disciplinarian that he was soon promoted to the principalship of one of the smaller schools of the city. His promotions followed rapidly into higher positions of trust and responsibility until he is now principal of the Dunbar School, which has been enlarged from a six to a twelve-room school since his encumbency. Prof. Grimes enjoys the confidence of all his work and stands for the natural ability and energy he has put in it.

S. J. Simpson

Mrs. S. J. Simpson

Residence of A. Z. Hester, 1702 West Street.

A. Z. Hester.

Mrs. A. Z. Hester.

Residence of Dr. E. B. Ramsey, 417 San Felipe Street.

W. H. Munroe and Family.

Dr. B. J. Covington and Residence, 2219 Dowling Street.

J. P. Sample and Family.

Residence of G. O. Burgess, Independence Heights.

G. O. Burgess, son of Alfred and Caroline Burgess of Millican, Brazos County, Texas. He was born in 1876, educated in the public free schools of the State. Was manager of his brother's drug-store in Bryan, Texas, and for several years conducted a successful grocery business of his own at Tamina, Tex.

By concentration and application he acquired a Normal education and for about eight years taught in the public free schools of the State. Took a course in law of the Sprague School of Law, Detroit, Mich.; was admitted to the bar and began the practice of law at Palestine, Texas, in 1906. Came to Houston in 1913, continuing his practice here, and became a resident citizen of Independence Heights.

Some years past was married to Miss Desdemona Bryant of Navasota, Tex., who is in all things an industrious and faithful wife. He is a member of Trinity M. E. Church, an active Mason and has from time to time been active in Republican politics. Was elected Mayor of Independence Heights by an overwhelming majority. Has a modest home in Independence Heights. Also owns some farm land in Montgomery County.

G. O. Burgess, Mayor of Independence Heights.

Mrs. G. O. Burgess and Sister, Mrs. Georgia Hall.

SOCIAL CALENDAR

Adkins, Mrs. John M. (nee Patsy D. Codwell—1869; 1218 O'Neil Street; phone Hadley 1423; former teacher; married in 1896 to John M. Adkins, Federal Court messenger; came to Houston 1901; student of public schools Navasota and Tillotson College. First colored girl to receive second grade State certificate; taught in Navasota City Schools eleven years. Member Antioch Baptist Church, Home Mission Society and Executive Board Kindergarten Association.

Black, Mrs. M. Augusta (nee Jackson)—1872; residence, 1323 Schwartz Street; phone Preston 9577; born in Nashville, Tenn.; came to Houston 1888; former occupation teacher; president Woman's Convention of Lincoln Southern Association; formerly secretary for six years. Member and S. S. teacher Friendship Baptist Church, Senior Usher Olive Leaf Sanctuary No. 39, A. O. O. P.

Bree, Mrs. Vicia—Housekeeper, 613 Robin Street. Member Bethel Baptist Church.

Bullock, Mrs. Hattie—Housewife, 3437 Tuam. Member Boynton Ch. M. E. Church.

Burton, Mrs. Irene (nee Thompson)—3020 McGowen Street; phone Hadley 2723. Member St. John's Baptist Church, Courts of Calanthe, S. P. No. 80, and secretary of Hester Court No. 57.

Bonner, Mrs. Melvina—1002 Palmer Street. Member Bethel Baptist Church, Olive Leaf Sanctuary, A. O. O. P., I. O. of Twelve, Assistant Recorder Hazel Tabernacle No. 89, K. & D. of T.

Burgess, Mrs. Desdemona W.—Wife of G. O. Burgess; is a daughter of Mr. and Mrs. Dennis Bryant. She was born and reared in Grimes County, Texas, near Navasota, where she attended the public schools. In a competitive examination she won a scholarship in Prairie View where she graduated with the class of 1903. She also attended one term at Bishop College. She has been an active teacher in the State before and after her marriage. She is now editress of the Independent Record, a newspaper published weekly in the interest of Independence Heights. She has been a consistent Christian for a number of years and now holds membership in Trinity M. E. Church. She is an active member of the Order of Eastern Star and holds the friendship of her sisters and neighbors. In her public career she has never ceased to be a careful housekeeper and devoted wife.

Calhoun, Mrs. Mary A.—Housewife, 624 Allston Street; phone Taylor 1484; born in Colorado County, Texas, and came to Houston 1904; public school education. Member of Damascus Baptist Church, I. G. Courts of Calanthe, K. of P., V. P. Charity Home, I. O. O. M. B.

Carr, Mrs. R. A.—Housewife, 1408 Travis Street; phone Preston 1387; born in Willis, Texas, and came to Houston 1913; graduate of Wiley University 1913. Member M. E. Church, President Woman's Home Missionary Society and Teacher S. S. Class.

Cooper, Mrs. Roxie (wife of Rev. C. C. Cooper)—600 Heiner Street; phone Preston 6960; native of Louisiana and came to Houston in 1904. Member and organist Friendship Baptist Church, 1906 Charity Club, A. O. O. P.

Crawford, Mrs Lucy—1848, born in Bexar County, Tex Member A M E Church, L O O F, K. of P

Dearing, Miss A K—Masseuse dermatologist phone Preston 6699, 1106 West St, native of Texas, graduate of Mary Allen College, came to Houston 1906, taught in public schools five years Member A M E Church, secretary K P, secretary Household of Ruth

Dickens Mrs S E—2905 Shepherd Street, born in Anderson, Texas, married W M Dickens in 1907. Member of St John s Baptist Church, secretary of Social Side Home Mission

Felder, Mrs A G—Housewife, 1605 Andrews Street, phone Preston 7950, native of Texas, came to Houston in 1906 Member Antioch Baptist Church, Household of Ruth and S M T

Ford, Mrs Gertrude—Housewife, 2210 St Charles Street Member Trinity M E Church, Deborah Chapter O E S, No 13

Ford, Mrs Jennie B—Housekeeper, 2616 Shepherd Street, native of Harris County Member of Baptist Church and Rose of Sharon Lodge No 12, A O O P

Grice Mrs Nancy—Housekeeper, 1312 Fiedrick Street Member Bethel Baptist Church, Missionary Worker for 16 years and member of U B F 20 years

Hagen, Mrs Annie (nee Mrs Butler, nee Miss Pruett)—1863, trained nurse and midwife, 609 Hobson Street phone Preston 6728, native Texan, came to Houston in 1889, first married to Mr Butler and by him has seven children, married in 1894 to Chas Hagen, retired, who was employed by the Merchants Compress for twenty years, first as fireman and then as assistant engineer, living issue of second marriage, one child Mrs Hagen is considered one of the best sick nurses and midwives in this section and gained her training and experience by working under several of the leading physicians of Houston She came to Houston with 50 cents and through her industry and thrift has accumulated a nice bit of property, owning her homestead and three rent houses, several city lots and farm property She organized the first nurses' training club and has trained up several colored nurses She has an Experienced Trained Nurse certificate Member of Friendship Baptist Church, Household of Ruth, Rose of Sharon Lodge No 12, A O O P

Harris, Mrs C L—Housewife, born in Wharton County, Texas, and came to Houston in 1909, married to C G Harris Member Antioch Baptist Church, property in Independence Heights attended Seguin College and received a Seamstress diploma

Harris Miss Charlina—1902, student at Little Rock, Ark Member of Church of God Her father, C G Harris, is one of Houston's leading photographers

Harmon, Mrs Hannah P—Housewife, 1012 Meyer Street born in Houston, graduate of Houston Industrial College 1900 Member Bethel Baptist Church, Household of Ruth No 219, and Grand Order of G U O O F

Hester, Mrs A Z (nee Julia C Thomas)—Housewife, 1703 West Street, phone Preston 5966 She is a native of Georgia and came to Houston in 1893 Student of Selman Seminary 1889-1890 Formerly school teacher Member Wesley A M E Church.

Past Grand Matron and present Grand Secretary of the State for the Order of the Heroines of Jericho, having held office in the State Order for ten years, also member of the Household of Ruth No 197 Nineteen and Six Art Club and Married Ladies' Social Art Club

Holden, Mrs Mary J (nee Mary Breedlove)—Teacher, 2917 Turner Street, phone Hadley 2192, native of Tuskegee, Alabama, graduate of Tuskegee 1903, came to Houston 1909 Mrs Holden has been teaching for nine years and now occupies the position of teacher of Domestic Science and Art in the High School Member Wesley A M E Church

Jones, Mrs D L—1879, housewife, 3115 Bear Street, born Houston Member Sloan Memorial M E Church, Treasurer of same, member and Treasurer S M T, member and Worthy Inspector Court of Calanthe, member of Household of Ruth

Kay, Mrs S G—1869, teacher, Harrisburg, Texas, R F D No 1, Box 323, born in Victoria County, Texas, teaching for 22 years Prior to coming to Harris County to take up her chosen work here Mrs Kay taught for several years in Victoria, Robertson and Montgomery counties where her work was characterized with excellence In 1909 she began her work at Harrisburg and four years later was made principal with a faculty of four teachers, and the building has been enlarged to a nice two-story, including four class rooms, domestic science and manual training departments Graduate of Prairie View Normal Member A M E Church, member Order of Ladies of Eastern Star, Secretary Adah A M W M and former Grand Martha, Superintendent Sunday School and District Superintendent of Epworth League in her church

Kennard, Mrs E S—Teacher, 1009 Robin Street, phone Preston 9115, born Fort Bend County, Texas, educated in Bishop College Marshall Taught school in Fort Bend County, Texas, for several years and is now teaching in Booker T Washington School Worthy Counsellor Olive Branch Court No 25, and Secretary of Theola Sanctuary No 301, member Bethel Baptist Church

Lee, Alice—Professional caterer, 208 Andrews Street, phone Preston 5464 Has followed occupation for twenty-four years Member Trinity M E Church

McNeil, Mrs T J—Housekeeper, 903 Cleveland Street Member St Paul's A M E Church, Sisters of Mysterious Ten and True Workers Temple No 228

McCullough, Mrs Olletta B—1881, housewife, 1318 Cleveland Street, graduate of Houston High School 1901 taught in public schools for three years Member and teacher in Sunday School Bethel Baptist Church, also member of choir for 17 years, member Antioch Temple S M T Married 1906 to P H McCullough

Miller, Mrs Ada L—1873, housewife, 310 Robin Street, phone Preston 2762, born in New Orleans, La, married Prof W E Miller 1894, came to Houston 1894 Member of Antioch Baptist Church, W P of S M T, A O of P, 1906 Art and Charity Club, Secretary of Antioch Baptist Sunday School for 18 years

Miller, Miss Lillian E—1902, student, 310 Robin Street, phone Preston 2762, born in Houston Member of Antioch Baptist Church

Moore, Mrs Mary—1861, housekeeper, 202 Andrews Street, born Belton, Texas, and reared by foster white mother Member Wesley Chapel A M E Church, A O of P and K & D of T

Nelson, Mrs Viola L—1880 2409 Hadley Street, born at Galveston, teaching 16 years, at present principal of Eighth Street, Houston Heights, School Member Trinity M E Church Graduate of Corsicana High School, normal graduate Member Eastern Star, S M T, Ancient Order of Pilgrims Eight years Recording Secretary of same

Pratt, Mrs Sarah L—Seamstress, 208 Andrews Street, phone Preston 5164, born Columbia, Texas, formerly taught school in West Texas and Houston six years Member Trinity M E Church and Goddess of Hope Temple No 11, S M T

Paley, Mrs Consada A—1883, 1310 George Street, born Waller County, Texas, came to Houston 1901, graduate Waller County Public School 1900 Member Bethel Baptist Church member Household of Ruth and Olive Leaf Sanctuary and Sewing Club

Perkins, Mrs Ida—1870, 1311 Dowling, born Houston, Texas, graduate common school, housewife Member Mt Zion Missionary Baptist Church

Pullum, Mrs Emma—1886, housewife, 1319 Andrews Street, phone Preston 302, native of Mississippi, attended school in Columbus, Miss, came to Houston 1896, married 1890 in Louisiana to Rev N P Pullum Member Friendship Baptist Church and President of Ladies' Missionary Society of church

Robinson, Mrs Elnora—1882, 620 Allston Street; born Houston, housewife Member Watt's Chapel Baptist Church, member Daughters of Tabor No 333, I O O M B, Christian Union

Robinson, Mrs E G—1884, housewife, 613 Robin Street, born in Louisiana Member Bethel Baptist Church and Missionary Society

Russell, Mrs Cora—1889, 1707 Velasco Street, native of Louisiana, came to Houston in 1914, graduate of New Iberia Schools in 1904; housewife Member of Fourth Baptist Church, member Wise Ladies of the World No 43, and Household of Ruth No 2170

Simpson, Mrs Emma—1879, 1302 San Felipe Street, housewife born Wharton County, Texas, came to Houston in 1910 Member Mt Zion Baptist Church, member Knights and Daughters of Tabor Married in 1906 to S J Simpson

Washington, Mrs Patsy—1873, 1010 San Felipe Street, born in Louisiana, came to Houston in 1910 Member St Paul's A M E Church, S S Teacher, Stewardess, member Epworth League

White, Miss Annie M—1614 Sherman Street, school teacher, now teaching in Fred Douglass School, began teaching in 1899 Member Antioch Baptist Church, member of Household of Ruth No 197

Williams, Mrs Lillie—Dressmaker, 2806 Odin Avenue Member Baptist Church and Knights and Daughters of Tabor

Williams, Mrs Augusta A (nee Banks)—1888, native of Houston, residence, 1407 San Felipe Street Member Friendship Baptist Church, member Missionary Society Married in 1908 to Julius W Williams

Rev. C. C. Harper.

Miss Charlina Harris.

Wm. M. Scott.

Albert McMurray.

J. W. Williams.

Mrs. J. W. Williams.

Miss Cornelius O. Williams.

Henry N. Williams.

Mr. and Mrs. D. C. Calhoun.

Mr. and Mrs. C. R. Robinson.

Mr. and Mrs. Harris Burton.

Mr. and Mrs. J. G. Rusell.

Residence of W. C. Conway, 1720 Leeland Ave.

W. C. Conway and Family.

Residence of H. J. Mitchell, 1501 Farwell Street.

Mr. and Mrs. H. J. Mitchell.

MARKS OF PROGRESS

BLESSING IN DISGUISE.

Many thousands of the Afro-American race cursed the slavery that came to them because of their seizure in their native land, and their forced exile across the water, in vessels of the English pirates and traders of that time, and cursed their sale into bondage into the hands of the white planters of the South; but now they can look around them and see the wonderful blessings that have come to them in the way of advancement, education and intelligence and look back on that bondage which they once thought a cross and see in it a wonderful blessing in disguise. Their cross has become a crown of blessing.

It brought them to that land which is today, to them, a land of freedom and opportunity, to which the jungles of their native land and the barbarians now inhabiting them can in no wise be compared.

They see themselves a people placed in pleasant places compared to those occupied by their people in Africa. They are themselves enjoying a measure of freedom, peace and prosperity which the greatest of their people in Africa never dreamed of. They are as a new people in a new land.

NO DISGRACE.

They did not come here of their own free will, yet who doubts but that, if they had had the foresight to see their race as it is today, they would not have voluntarily come over and served in "bondage for a season" that their children might reap the benefits of this wonderful country and government of ours? Most all nations known to mankind have, at one time or other, been in vassalage to a stronger nation. The Christ Himself was born a slave or vassal of the Romans, so that there is no disgrace attached to having been born a slave or a son of a slave.

JEHOVAH DESIGNS.

The great Jehovah has designed that some skins be brown, some black, some white, some red and some yellow. The color of the skin has nothing to do with the characteristics. It is no more a disgrace to have a black skin than it is to have a skin of any other color. The disgrace for any race is to have a black heart.

AS A CHILD.

The Afro-Americans were brought to this country and sold into bondage as a little babe, unlearned and untutored. As a child babbling a strange tongue they landed in a strange land and took up the white man's burden and for about two centuries they bore the white man on their backs. After emancipation for a long period of reconstruction and rehabilitation the white man carried the black man on his back. Now, however, neither race has to bear the other on its back for the Afro-American race is gradually finding its industrial life and reaching its commercial independence.

A HARD WORK

As it is there are millions of the race today who deplore and hate the life and works of the low, vicious element of their race as much as does the most refined of any race The Afro-American has a work to do in struggling to eliminate this vicious element, which is of stupendous onerousness It is a fight and a burden before which many a stronger race might well quail Thousands are consecrating their every energy to the work, hopefully and prayerfully, feeling that the stain must be removed from their garments

As the white races have led them into temptation, in the long gone past, it is now up to those same nations to assist in eradicating the stench it helped so to make

INTELLIGENCE VS BARBARIANISM

Take away the intelligence that has been our heritage and our guide for the past few centuries and you place us all back where we were as barbarians of the dark ages This intelligence which means all the difference between the best men of today and the worst barbarians of 6,000 years ago, has been vouchsafed to the members of the Afro-American race, so that today they are enjoying the largest degree of freedom from fetishism and from ignorance and superstition ever enjoyed by a race so similarly situated and so shortly come from among peoples of utter darkness

HELPING HAND

The "helping hand" must be credited for this state of affairs They have been helped and the larger number of the race appreciate it and are not only helping themselves but are striving to pay back the benefactor with a worthy life and with service so needful to the peace and prosperity of this country

Although racially far apart, geographically the races are together, so, through no will of their own, the Afro-Americans find themselves in these United States, the country of their adoption, able to make their progress heard through their industrial and allied lines, in no small way

ADVANCE EDUCATIONALLY

In no other way has the Afro-American race shown its progress more clearly than in the decreased percentage of illiteracy since 1870 Taking the country as a whole the number of illiterates, that is, those over ten years old who cannot read or write, was 45 for each hundred, in 1870 Today the percentage of illiterates is 24 out of each hundred This is 6 less per hundred than the illiterates of foreigners in America The number of illiterates of Afro-Americans living in towns and cities in 1870 was 82 out of each hundred It is now less than 18 to the hundred, or a decrease of nearly one-half If the present decrease of illiteracy continues among the members of the Afro-American race it will entirely disappear by 1940

If this proves any one fact more than another it proves that the Afro-Americans are availing themselves to the utmost of the privilege of an education

By reference to the article on "Efficiency" by Emmett J Scott you will see the wonderful progress made in the establishing of schools for the race in the United States It is not necessary to repeat this information in this article I only wish to call your attention strongly to the fact that the illiteracy is decreasing at a faster rate among the Afro-Americans than it is among the whites of America   While the figures are away above those of the white race, still the decrease is more marked

ATTENDANCE ON SCHOOLS

When it comes to the actual per cent of those within the school age who are in attendance on schools the Afro-Americans reach nearly to fifty per cent, or one-half of the whole number   The record for foreigners shows but 31 per cent in attendance

LOCAL PERCENTAGE ON ILLITERACY

It is gratifying to know that Houston has a very low percentage of illiteracy as compared with other cities of like size in the United States, which speaks well for the standing of the race in this city   While the average for the United States, of city population, among the Afro-Americans is nearly 18 per cent of illiteracy the per cent of illiterates in Houston is only about 16

GAINFUL OCCUPATIONS

Just a little summary gives the facts as to gainful occupations among the Afro-Americans as compared with the native whites of the United States

The number of native whites, males engaged in gainful pursuits is 78 5 for each hundred   That of Afro-Americans, males, is 87 4 for each hundred   The per cent of female native whites is 17 1 per hundred and the per cent of Afro-Americans, females, engaged in gainful pursuits is 54 7 per hundred

Of the Afro-Americans in Texas 54 9 females and 86 7 males out of each hundred are engaged in gainful pursuits

By far the greater number in all parts of the United States are engaged in agricultural pursuits   In Texas 92 4 males and 93 4 females out of each hundred, from the ages of 10 years and up to 15, who are engaged in making a living are classed as agriculturists that is, engaged in agriculture and kindred lines

As the list grows larger through addition of those who are older, this percentage shrinks somewhat

POPULATION OF TEXAS CITIES

The Afro-American population of the seven largest cities of Texas as given in the 1910 census shows Houston, 23,929, Dallas, 18,024, Fort Worth, 13,280, San Antonio, 10,716 Galveston, 8,036, Austin, 7,478, Waco, 6,067

However, it is evident that the population of several of these cities is far in advance of these figures for the Afro-American race It is estimated that Houston has 30,000 Afro-Americans in round numbers

The population of Harris County is from 25 to 37½ per cent Afro-American, while about one-seventh of the farmers of the county belong to that race

TEXAS

The population of Afro-Americans in Texas has increased from 490,000 in 1890 to about 700,000 in 1915, or an increase of nearly ten thousand per year. As compared with the foreigners in Texas the Afro-Americans are nearly three to one. Population of foreigners, 242,000.

FOREIGN BORN

Less than one in two hundred of the Afro-Americans in the United States is foreign born while taking the white races as a whole one in eight is foreign born.

As compared with the foreigners the Afro-Americans have a much better grade of literacy. The average Afro-American illiteracy is 24 per cent, the average of those in cities is 17 9, the average of foreigners in cities is 21 2, the average of Afro-Americans in rural districts is 27 3, while the average for foreigners is 34. This makes a total average for the Afro-Americans as aforesaid of 24 per cent and a total average for foreigners of 30 per cent. The illiteracy for Afro-Americans in 1870 was 32 per cent, or nearly one-third, who did not know how to read or write, while only 3-17ths are now illiterate in the cities, and this is rapidly being cut down.

The record shows that 57 per cent of the Afro-Americans are married, this is the average of all races in the United States.

The increase in farmers of Afro-American race in Texas for the last ten years has been at the rate of 500 per year.

Of course, when one race makes up about 7 24ths of the population of a city the size of Houston it is reasonable to suppose that a considerable portion of the commercial and industrial life and work of that city is due and done by and through that 7 24ths.

That Houston is no exception to this conclusion, but that on the other hand it emphasizes this very fact in its record of industrial and commercial life among its Afro-American citizenship, is well attested in the list that is given in the back of this book, to which your attention is called.

It is impossible to denote the amount of money invested in any particular line of endeavor or to get at the total in any way as no separate record is given.

CHURCH ORGANIZATIONS AND PASTORS

Antioch Missionary Baptist Church—313 Robin   Rev. F L Lights, Pastor

Apostolic Faith Mission—813 W 22d Avenue, Houston Heights

Bee Bee Tabernacle C M E Church—San Felipe and Arthur   Rev W Q Hunter, Pastor

Bethel Baptist Church—801 Andrews

Boynton Chapel M E Church—1120 Paige Rev Jesse W Gilder, Pastor

Brown's Chapel A M E Church—3208 Washington   Rev P C Hunt, Pastor

Burrell's Baptist Church—1104 Sampson   Rev Jes Covington, Pastor

Calvary M. E Church—Dowling   Rev W E Kelly, Pastor

Calvary Baptist Church—320 Sampson

Camp Zion Baptist Church—99 Pless, Rev Charles H Smith, Pastor

Christian Home Missionary Baptist Church—Anderson, southeast corner Scott   Rev B J Leroy, Pastor

Church of Living God—Corner Velasco and McGowen   Rev A McDonald Pastor

Church of God in Christ—Corner Railroad and Oliver

Church of God—1020 Saulnier   Rev James Pendleton, Pastor

Cottage Grove Baptist Church—North side M K & T west of Detering

Damascus Baptist Church—1114 Sampson   Rev John Covington, Pastor

Damascus Baptist Church—1109 Court   Rev. D H Rankin, Pastor

Emanuel Missionary Baptist Church—817 Herkimer, Houston Heights   Rev T J Hardeman, Pastor

Daughters of Zion Baptist Church—One block north of Washington, one block west of Detering

First True Vine Baptist Church—Corner White Oak and Tietam Place   Rev Frank Walker, Pastor

Fourth Missionary Baptist Church—1101 Dowling Rev Herbert B. Southern, Pastor

Friendship Missionary Baptist Church—702 San Felipe   Rev N P Pullum, Pastor

Gallilee Missionary Baptist Church—2811 Montgomery Road   Rev John Robinson, Pastor

Good Hope Missionary Baptist Church—1402 Saulnier Rev C H Hunt, Pastor

Gospel Hill Baptist Church—Whitty, three blocks north of 9th   Rev B M Williams, Pastor

Holiness Church of Christ—No regular pastor Services every Sunday at 1709 Robin

Jerusalem Missionary Baptist Church—2805 Hutchins   Rev J H Makey, Pastor

Jordan Grove Baptist Church—Dowling and Gray   Rev J R Lofton, Pastor

Little Damascus Baptist Church—One block west of Reinerman, between Pine and Buffalo Bayou   Rev William Sykes, Pastor

Little Zion Baptist Church—Velasco and Wilson   Rev Gilbert Green, Pastor

Lively Hope Baptist Church—31 Schrimpf   No regular pastor

Macedonia Baptist Church—1216 Ruthven   No regular pastor

Macedonia Missionary Baptist Church—1006 Ruthven   Rev J W Edwards, Pastor

Macedonia Missionary Baptist Church—2901 Whitty   Rev C J W. Boyd, Pastor

Mt Airy Baptist Church—1709 Robin

Mallalieu Chapel M E Church—1918 Hickory   Rev R H. Warren, Pastor

McGowen Chapel C M E Church—South side Green, two blocks east of Benson   Rev Amos J Wolf, Pastor

Mt Calvary Baptist Church—718 Shepherd   Rev Wm M Guy, Pastor

Mt Corinth Baptist Church—924 Schwartz   Rev Sauls, Pastor

Mt Olive Baptist Church—103 Denver   Rev Matthew H Ellis, Pastor

Mt Olive Baptist Church—602 Meadow   Rev John Brantford, Pastor

Mt. Pilgrim Missionary Baptist Church—3608 Main   Rev. Charles H Smith Pastor

Mt Pillar Missionary Baptist Church—601 Hemphill   Rev R L Williams, Pastor

Mt Pleasant Baptist Church—2713 Liberty   Rev J J James, Pastor

Mt Pleasant Free Missionary Baptist Church—South side Telephone Road, one mile east of Dumble

Mt Rose Missionary Baptist Church—519 Rutland. Houston Heights   Rev John W Craig, Pastor

Mt Sinai Missionary Baptist Church—725 Railroad, Houston Heights. Rev W M Jones, Pastor

Mt Vernon M. E Church—2727 Burnett   Rev J I Gilmore, Pastor

Mt Zion Baptist Church—2310 German   Rev E H Branch, Pastor

Mt Zion Missionary Baptist Church—835 W 23d, Houston Heights   Rev G R Alford, Pastor

Nazarene Missionary Baptist Church—Three blocks south of San Felipe, half mile west of G H & S A Ry   Rev D H Hawkins, Pastor

New Bethel Baptist Church—2318 Ann   Rev Wm Treadville, Pastor

New Birth Baptist Church—44 N E Broadway.   Rev Alexander Farris, Pastor

New Hope Baptist Church—3718 Broadway   Rev A T Gordon, Pastor

New Hope Baptist Church—1221 Crockett   Rev C B Williams, Pastor

New Mt Calvary Church—2923 Richardson   Rev Wm Rice, Pastor

New Mt. Moriah Church—3113 Baer   Rev Warner T Perry, Pastor

New Mt Pilgrim Baptist Church—3405 St Charles   Rev W H Rhodes, Pastor

New Zion Baptist Church—1316 Ovid   Rev W R Mays, Pastor

Old Land Mark Baptist Church—West end W 14th Avenue, Houston Heights   Rev J W Austin, Pastor

Payne Chapel A M E Church—1517 Hill   Rev O L Bonner, Pastor

Pilgrim Congregationalist Church—1422 Wilson   Rev M F Foust, Pastor

Pine Grove Baptist Church—Galveston and Holman   Rev L L Nelson, Pastor

Pleasant Grove Baptist Church—2802 Opelousas   Rev N T Lane, Pastor

Red Rose Primitive Baptist Church—West side Meadow, three blocks south Roanoke   Rev W M Rice, Pastor

St James M E Church—302 Andrews   Rev C H Holden, Pastor

St John Baptist Church—2104 Broadway   Rev Wm Johnson, Pastor

St John Baptist Church—Corner Dowling and McGowen   Rev H R Johnson Pastor

St Mark A M E Church—One block east of Detering and two and one-half blocks north of Buffalo Bayou   Rev Lewis Martin, Pastor

St Mark Missionary Baptist Church—58 I & G N. Place   Rev W H Snow, Pastor

St Matthew's Baptist Church—Velasco, northeast corner Fulton Avenue   Rev J E Edwards, Pastor

St Nicholas Catholic Church—1018 Chenevert   Rev Wm Murphy, Pastor

St Paul M E Church—1710 Edwards   Rev. J L Mosely, Pastor

Second Baptist Church of Houston Heights—840 W 20th   Rev A D Foster, Pastor

Second Pleasant Green Baptist Church—South side Cleveland one block west of Beecher   Rev Wm E Smith, Pastor

Seventh Day Adventist Church—1310 George   Rev J W Johnson, Pastor

Shiloh Baptist Church—2914 Providence   Rev C W Holmes, Pastor

Sloan Memorial M E Church—3102 Nance   Rev W H Jackson, Pastor

Sunlight Chapel Baptist Church—3515 Columbia   Rev Roy Amos, Pastor

Sweet Home Missionary Baptist Church—3420 Broadway   Rev Williams, Pastor

Trinity M E Church—1412 Travis   Rev A W Carr, Pastor

Truevine Baptist Church—1901 Whitty   Rev C J W Boyd, Pastor

Wayman Chapel A M E Church—802 W 20th Avenue, Houston Heights

Wesley Chapel A M E Church—2201 Dowling   Rev E J Howard, Pastor

Residence of T. Hogrobrooks, 809 19th Ave., Houston Heights.

Mr. and Mrs. T. Hogrobrooks.

Residence of D. B. McMillan, 2216 Gray Avenue.

Joseph H. Jackson, Contractor and Builder

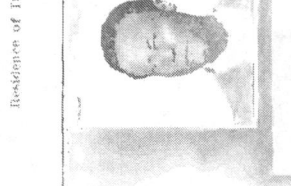

Mr. and Mrs. D. B. McMillan

A. J. Johnson, Contractor and Builder

Residence of James Kyle, 526 Hobson St.

Residence of Will Luckey, 3102 Turner Street.

Residence of Mr. and Mrs. S. M. Nelson, 2109 Hadley Avenue

Electric Indicator.

NED EASTMAN BARNES.

Ned Eastman Barnes was born in Waller County, Texas, in 1868, and received his education at the public schools. In 1884 he was married to Miss Ada Johnson of Willis, Texas. From this union has come three boys. Two of them are now teaching school, Fisher and Wheeler; and the third, James, is private secretary and assistant to his father. He followed the occupation of farming until his work as an inventor and promoter took all of his time. He came to Houston in 1913, and has devoted his time since in promoting several meritorious propositions. He has a well improved and well stocked farm of 160 acres, and has so far received a good sum of money for the work of his brain in inventions. Two of his inventions are seen on this page. These are the railway track brace to prevent the spreading of rails, and the electric indicator for giving the time of arrival and leaving of trains through a moving picture screen. Other inventions are the station bulletin board, a hot box cooler and oiler, a sand band, a combination table and meat block, and a stove pipe lock. Mr. Barnes is a member of Farmers' Improvement Society of Willis, Texas; member of A. M. Silver Seal No. 182, Willis, Texas, and K. of P., Rodgers No. 144. He is a deacon of the Baptist church and superintendent of the Sunday School.

Railway Track Brace.

An Address Delivered by Hon. W. M. C. Dickson, of Houston, on the Occasion of Emancipation Celebration

Ladies and Gentlemen —

I congratulate you upon this healthy and imposing demonstration in due commemoration of that historic event which forty-eight years ago broke the shackles which bound you, your father and my father in chattel bondage It is very fitting that you should do this The splendid pageant in which you have engaged but shows to the world that you know how to be grateful for that which to you has been a benefit or blessing This alone should win for you the respect and admiration of peoples more fortunate than we, because it argues convincingly that you will not forget a friend who has been friendly, and that with due ceremony and appreciation you will hand down to posterity the cherished memory of events and men which have contributed to the righteous evolution of a great race In this you are not unlike the other great races of earth, and in no less degree may be called men For ever since humanity has evolved from a primitive and semi-barbarous state, there has existed within the human breast admiration for the spectacular, the daring and the sublime Whatever the stage of mental development or moral susceptibility, the human spirit has been known to leap from its circumscribed bounds to worship at the shrine of a saint, to stand in wonderment and awe before a masterpiece of art, to feel the thrill of emulation for him who has dared to do a righteous though unpopular act

This emulation may not lead one to court a martyr's death, to brave the torture of the stake, or to rejoice while locked in perpetual night in a felon's dungeon, as many heroes of the past have done For, though one would escape these ghastly and painful experiences, though we make no outward demonstration betraying sympathy or approval in instances where justice has been trampled under foot and the innocent woefully persecuted, there is, nevertheless, deep down in the human sensibilities a sympathy for the oppressed, admiration for the hero, approval of the right

This is the saving element of the human race This is the leaven which makes the moral tendency of the age always upwards

The world at every stage is growing better, each decade brings and has brought human society nearer and nearer to that state in which every man will respect the rights and feelings of every other, and when every man will know that the highest welfare of all is best secured by promoting the highest welfare of every race or individual The wave of human events swings ever onward and not backward The movement is progression and not retrogression

True it is that individuals go backwards Races and nations become extinct when surrounded by conditions to which they can not adjust themselves or to which their natures do not respond, but human society the world over has attained unto a more advanced state, the eternal purposes of the Creator have been more nearly realized

Turmoil and strife, wars and conquest but betray that filtering evolutionary process by which that which is weak, unjust or corruptible is swept away to make room for that which is higher and fitter Yea, the good may sometimes fall, the weak may often be unjustly persecuted, today may break the peace and tranquility of yesterday, plague and famine may today devastate the rich and populous territory of yesterday but as a wave upon the mighty ocean swings now up, now down, but whose course is ever onward with a slow majestic motion, so the drift of human events has been ever towards a more perfect state, though one day may shatter the hopes of the day before and turn the veriest order into seeming chaos

The human spirit is free and cannot intrinsically tolerate slavery, though that same being may enslave another, the human conscience cannot approve of injustice, though the same individual may persecute a fellowman the human sense of honesty and fair dealing cannot applaud corruption, though the very person may enrich himself with the spoils of graft, and hence, when slavery, injustice and corruption sweep men on to the verge of depravity and perdition, the soul of the nation rises in righteous revolt, shakes off the fetters of littleness and sin leaps over the confines of decadence and death, and comes forth in a purer and higher state

Every great event that has accelerated this movement towards higher and better things has left its imprint upon human annals, written not alone on books or parchment, the memory of which serves to quicken human activity in the cause of truth, and to bring the ultimate triumph of right into planer view

We do right, therefore to assemble upon the anniversary of such events, and with due ceremony commemorate their occurrence The memory of them cannot but have a saving effect upon the minds of succeeding generations, they appeal to the highest sentiment of the soul and lift the thoughts to sublimer and nobler things

A race or nation can be trusted to shape its own destinies so long as hero worship is considered a virtue, and epoch-making events receive due and just consideration, for the noble traits, the great and inspiring deeds which look to the betterment of the world, the mighty and potent happenings which have shaken the world in the cause of right, cannot but have a saving influence upon the minds and doings of men, and therefore cause them to walk in paths of rectitude and discretion The individual, the family, the State shall alike feel this wholesome effect, and shall accordingly guard their steps lest they too, might drop into the pitfalls that have brought many men and nations to an inglorious end

Every surviving race or nation has had its inspiring events Every great cause that has withstood the tossing tempests of time has its adherents who look with pride and reverence upon the past and feel more secure because of what they have met and overcome The heart of every Britisher burns with pride as he points to the destruction of the Spanish Armada which made Great Britain supreme upon the seas, and made possible the triumph of English commerce and civilization throughout the world The adherents to the Christian religion reverence as saintly the memory of Charles Martell, whose good sword checked the advance of Saracenic hosts in Southern Europe and thus prevented the spread of Mohammedanism over all that country and consequently to America And why may not Americans, regardless of color or race, cherish the memory of Lincoln and the Emancipation Proclamation that saved the country from disintegration and death, and delivered all Americans from the thralldom of a bondage more deadly than mere chattel slavery?

The Negro race, whose estate was changed from that of an animal to a man, can celebrate no event more pregnant with possibilities for the future than the receiving of the Emancipation Proclamation nor can it pay homage to any greater character than Abraham Lincoln The memory of these upon this anniversary day should stir the sublimest emotions in the soul of every Negro who loves mankind and his race He is worse than a traitor who would calumniate so great a character as Abraham Lincoln or deny the far-reaching potency of his statesmanship

There are those who say that Lincoln freed the slaves not because he loved them or thought the black man the equal of the white man, but that he did it only as a measure incident to the saving of the Union True it is that Lincoln loved his country more than he loved the slave, and sought first to save his country at all hazards. But it is equally true that Lincoln hated slavery and looked only for an opportunity when he could consistently deal it a death blow The question of whether the black man was the equal of the white man as a social being did not enter in It is true, however, that Lincoln did not regard the black man the white man's equal, the black man, enthralled with a bondage one hour of which said Thomas Jefferson, was fraught with more misery than ages of that which occasioned the War of the Revolution, the white man free and master of his own destinies, the one groping in ignorance and degradation because of his bondage, the other aristocratic and courting the learning and refinement of the world, the one with no ancestry save the semi-savage inhabitants of the Dark Continent, the other pointing with pride to a long line of blue blood traceable to European nobility Is it reasonable, then to suppose that Lincoln, himself a white man thought the Negro his own equal as a man ? Not so but Lincoln thought that the black man, degraded and lowly as he was, deserving of an equal chance in the struggle for existence as the white man, that the black man had just as much right to love home and family and to cherish sacred ties as the white man, that the black man has an immortal soul which must account to its God as well as the white man

This was the thought that burned itself into the soul of the great emancipator and made him dare to give the Negro a man's chance in the world, and this is the heritage that we received at his mighty hands This is what emancipation meant to the Negro when the shackles were broken, and this is what it means today. It was then that we came to the parting of the ways, and the choice of the way that we are to pursue will determine whether or not we shall be numbered among the surviving races and bearing our portion of the burden of the world's civilization, one way leading through rainbow-like visions that change and fade every moment, through dreams and fancies which, like the flickering will-o-the-wisp that lures the traveler on into the pathless swamp where bogs and quicksands await his inexperienced feet, vanish from sight, leaving us in darkness, on the verge of despair and far away from the high plains of usefulness and success, the other way rock-paved and leading ever upwards through the foothills and mountains of obstacle and difficulty where with tug and struggle we clamber over the cliffs of high endeavor and stand at last upon the mountain top of achievement

The followers of the first way are those who saw no difference between liberty and license, who used their first free days in the pursuit of hurtful pleasures, indulging all the while in misguided notions of the rights and privileges of a free man, and finally ending up in poverty, crime and in many cases a death in ignominy, while the followers of the second way are those who toiled through the night that the following day might not be one of failure and want, who were content with small things until by struggle and privation they had achieved greater, who thought upon higher things and modeled their ways in accordance with honesty and truth

The right to choose our own way and thus work out our own destiny was what emancipation meant to the slave and what it was intended to mean by the immortal Lincoln

And who will deny that this is the correct view ? What care we today whether the proud Anglo-Saxon considers us his equal, if he will only accord to us an equal opportunity to work out our own destiny in the great activities of life? As we drift down the avenue of life our watchword is not "social equality" but "opportunity," opportunity to help develop the resources of this vast country and to have an unhindered share in helping to direct its mighty economic forces Let us be given this chance, and it must inevitably follow that all questions of a purely social nature will be happily adjusted It is meet therefore, that we honor the name of Lincoln, and cherish the memory of the statesman who could look down the future and see so great possibilities for a race yet denied the right of being men

And while we look backwards with reverence and veneration, we would not forget that the call of the age is "forward" The problems of the future are more momentous and exacting than those of the past Being as we are an infant race just going forth to survive or perish in the world's great drama of life, how careful should we be! How grave must be the situation when but the next step may lead us into irretrievable error!

Politicians and scholars of other races have devoted much time to the drawing out of theories applicable to the so-called race problem in America Scholars and divines of our own race have disagreed and argued vehemently over the best way by which the Negro may attain the highest mission which we believe he is destined to perform The questions concerning personal freedom were less refractory than those which we must now meet concerning our own industrial and economic freedom The giving of the Negro political power was a problem less grave than that pertaining to his highest function as a political factor And as we theorize and ponder upon these things, we are often too forgetful that individual character is the first great essential to success and accomplishment in any undertaking or aspiration The honest, unselfish, peaceful citizen who wishes all men well, and who regards it as much his duty to guard the interests of others as those of himself, will succeed, and it is only he of such character who will achieve any large measure of success The man who will filch from the man with whom he deals that which rightfully belongs to him because he is not looking, will betray his country or his race The man who will falsify the truth for any temporary advantage in the social or commercial world is a rotten pillar in our racial structure and if the race is made up of such our whole racial fabric is doomed to disintegration and death The individual whose acts will not stand the test of the unchanging principles of truth, has not the elements of success in him and is a failure now

Look around us and see who are those who are succeeding permanently They are those who are trusted because proven trustworthy, they are those who are served by others because themselves serving and willing to serve, those made leaders because willing themselves to follow Let each man, therefore, look to himself, for as the individual or the majority of individuals, so the race

And notwithstanding the theories and dissertations of scholars and divines, I say there is no problem, we are only in the midst of a condition that requires an awakening Two things must concur to cure the racial situation in America—individual character on the one hand and opportunity on the other The one devolves upon us, the other devolves most largely upon those among whom we live

Let us, therefore, imbibe the true emancipation spirit, the times and conditions challenge us to be brave industrious, vigilant and just And let every man who has faith in Jehovah and the eternal fitness of things live his highest life, let his everyday acts give expression to his highest self, taking counsel from the lessons of the past, and trusting in the one unchanging God, to whom alone the future belongs, we know that all is well

PROF. ROBERT M. CATCHINGS.

Prof. Robert M. Catchings, residence 2618 Rice Street. Phone Hadley 3441. Born at Lynchburg, Texas, and came to Houston in 1888. Graduate of Prairie View Normal, taking the industrial and normal courses. Took Post Graduate course at Bradley Polytechnic Institute of Peoria, Ill., and spent some time inspecting the manual training schools of Chicago and St. Louis. Formerly Assistant Principal Hempstead High School and now instructor of Manual Training in Houston High School. Teaching ten years, of which six years have been spent as teacher in Houston High School. Member Mt. Zion Baptist Church, also clerk of church. Member and Grand Lodge Representative of K. of P.; proprietor of a grocery store run by wife and clerk. Married to Bessie G. Maynard in 1913. One child, Maynard Catchings, born October, 1914. Owns five-acre plot near city and home and store on corner lot at residence.

THE TEXAS FREEMAN.

The Texas Freeman, the only secular newspaper owned, controlled and operated by Negroes in Houston, is a weekly publication, issued regularly each week at 409½ Milam Street by Charles Norvell Love, editor, publisher and owner. It is not a corporation nor partnership. It is an individual enterprise and is owned and controlled absolutely by the present management that has issued it each Saturday since November 1, 1902, enabling it to be independent in politics and everything else save and except its racial interest.

The Texas Freeman is justly styled the organ and tribune of the Negro race whose cause it espouses fearlessly, come what may, sink or swim. It is the *rade mecum* of a most discriminating clientele, and it speaks out on all occasions, defining its position positively, so that those who run may read.

Charles N. Love, the editor, is a native Texan. He was born at Washington, in Washington County, Texas, September 22, 1862, coming to Houston with his mother, Mrs. Sarah Jane Holland, deceased, and his two brothers, William and Richard, in August, 1865, immediately after emancipation, where he resided continuously, except at intervals, when he resided in Grimes County, between Courtney and Navasota, until November, 1885, when he took up residence permanently in Houston.

Editor Love, as everybody calls him, has been active in public life since he was 18 years old. He has been prominent in all civic and political affairs and has been a factor socially and industrially all the while, standing up conspicuously always, looming largely on Houston's horizon.

He was married to Miss Lilla Branch Sunday evening, December 7, 1902, his married life being a happy wedded existence, he and his better half being equally mated and matched, the couple together having acquired their proportionate share of this world's goods.

Editor Love belongs to the "well-to-do" class of the colored population. He owns his business and he owns his home and in addition to these he owns improved and unimproved property in the Third and Fourth Wards, lots in Independence Heights and in Sunny Side Place and acreage in Highland Acre Homes and in the Lincoln Farms Addition, all free and unencumbered, and operates on a cash basis.

Mr. and Mrs. C. G. Harris.

HENRY L. MIMS.

Henry Lucius Mims was born in Bryan, Brazos County, Texas, August 13, 1874. He attended the public schools of that city for a period of ten years and was graduated from the Bryan High School in the class of 1890. He afterwards taught two terms in city schools of Bryan, and at the same time specialized in History and Mathematics under private white instructors. He was appointed a substitute railway postal clerk in April, 1893. In September of same year he received his probationary appointment to the line of the Houston & Texas Central Railway, his permanent appointment following three months later. He has been promoted successively from the lowest grade at $800 per annum to the highest at $1,700 per annum, which is the highest point any clerk may reach in the ranks. He is the only Negro clerk in charge of a crew in a Class "C" line in Texas, save one.

He is a member of the A. M. E. Church and has been chorister of the choir for eight years. He is also a member of the K. of P. fraternity. He was the founder and first National President of the National Alliance of Postal Employees.

NATIONAL ALLIANCE OF POSTAL EMPLOYEES.

The National Alliance of Postal Employees, an organization designed to protect the rights and privileges of Negroes in the Postal Service, was originally projected and fostered by the Negro Railway Postal Clerks in Houston, Texas. As soon as the Democratic administration of President Woodrow Wilson went into power, an agitation began among some persons in the postal service having for its object the curtailment of the privileges of the Negroes employed in this service.

The agitation became so strong till it was thought that many Negroes would be summarily dismissed from the service, others reduced in grade, and still others humiliated by practices which were suggested to the officials by certain organizations of white employees, such practices designed to place Negroes in the smaller and less important assignments. To offset this agitation and take steps to protect their interests, a meeting was held in Houston composed of the best thought amongst the Negro clerks of this city. The meeting was suggested by Clerks Mims, Patten, Sweatt, Young and others, who finally got the men together for the first time in the office of T. H. Fairchild, a former clerk who had resigned and was in the real estate business. This meeting was held May 12, 1913, at 7:30 p. m., and was attended by Clerks Mims, Sweatt, Brown, Taylor, Keeling, Young, Dodson, Robinson, Glover, Rutledge, Southwell, Smith, Jessie. Sloan, Jones, Ayres, Patten.

From this meeting grew the Progressive Postal League, which concern projected the Chattanooga convention which founded the National Alliance of Postal Employees. Henry L. Mims was elected temporary president of the first meeting in Houston; T. R. Brown, secretary; J. L. Sweatt, treasurer. At the Chattanooga meeting Henry L. Mims was elected national president; R. L. Bailey of Indiana, secretary; A. H. Hendricks of Georgia, treasurer; C. B. Shepperson of Arkansas, vice-president; B. H. Holerman of Louisiana, editor. H. L. Mims and M. B. Patten of Houston and J. R. Thomas of San Antonio were delegates to the Chattanooga meeting. The same clerks with G. N. T. Gray of Ft. Worth and J. M. Richardson of Denison, Tex., were representatives to the St. Louis convention in 1914, which re-elected Mims president for a second term.

The organization is now in a prosperous condition and is recognized as the spokesman for the Negro railway postal clerks by the Postoffice Department.

Residence of E. W. Robinson, 1504 Dowling St.

Residence of T. R. Brown, 2412 Dowling St.

Officers and Members of the Second Annual Convention of the National Alliance of Postal
Employees at Houston, Texas, July 23-27, 1915

Residence of Mrs. Annie Hagen, 609 Hobson Street

Property of Mrs. Annie Hagen, 611 Hobson Street

Prof. R. H. Lockett   Dr. E. A. Durham.   W. M. C. Dickson, Attorney.

Mr. and Mrs. W. M. Dickens.

John T. Stafford.

Mrs. John T. Stafford.

B. C. Robinson.

Mr. and Mrs. E. T. Noble.

Rev. W. D. Hill.

James A. Hayward.

Rev. O. L. Bonner.

L. Washington.   James Williams.   J. G. Glenn.

Mr. and Mrs. P. H. McCullough.   Mr. and Mrs. A. D. Paley.

Sam Cebron.   Green Hogan.   Bailey McCoy.

DIGEST OF RULES OF ETIQUETTE

TRUE ETIQUETTE.

True etiquette is simply kind and true thought for the rights and accommodation of others. In other words, putting another's pleasure and delight before your own.

The child that is rightly brought up naturally acquires the ideas of true etiquette. To make a mistake in your social dealings with others and to lay it to ignorance, claiming that you did not know better, is as bad as to willfully disregard the feelings of others.

In order to be truly sincere and kind you must forget yourself oftentimes, in order to show your regard for others.

To be kind and considerate, to avoid anything that would bring offense in the least, and to guard your thoughts, words and feelings, so that no offense shall be given, constitutes the whole of true etiquette.

Good manners should begin at home. Because you happen to be at home with other members of your family, children, parents, brothers or sisters does not excuse you when you fail to show good manners. The home should build the foundation of your good manners and etiquette.

GOOD MANNERS.

Always lift your hat when talking to one in authority, or to your father, mother or sister, or when addressing a woman either in or out of the house, or when addressing elderly people.

Be as polite to another man, whether in your station or not, as you would have him to be with you.

Always address your relatives, friends and acquaintances with a polite "good morning," "evening" or "afternoon," and be sure to see that you do not slight a handshake if offered in friendship. You have no more right to offend by a slight than you have to offend by a blow.

Keep your good manners always right by avoiding evil communications, which corrupt good manners as taught by St. Paul.

Honor thy father and mother and return good for evil.

Be considerate of the feelings and rights of all other members of the family. It is not right or at all nice to try to make yourself officious, or to try to bulldoze even the least member of the family.

Be gentle in your speech. A loud mouth is no sign of brains or of courage.

Remember that good manners and politeness have led many a boy or girl up higher, and have ofttimes led to fortune and fame. And any boy or girl can have these whether they have anything else or not.

Remember that "good manners" can not be put on and off at pleasure. Manners that are "put on" are not the "good" kind. They must be part of you. They make up your nature, and if you find yourself able to put on or take them off at pleasure, be sure you have a bogus brand of manners.

Remember that a courteous word, a pleasant smile, or a polite bow, all of which costs nothing, may mean a great deal.

Remember that true courtesy comes from within, from a heart of genuine kindness, and does not consist of a silly smirk or a vain attempt to "show how nice you can be." You don't have to "show" true courtesy. It shows itself.

When doing a favor do not let it lose all its flavor by doing it with a "loud noise." Be unobtrusive in doing any favor.

PUBLIC MANNERS

A gentleman should never take a lady's arm

A gentleman should not speak unless the lady speaks first

A gentleman should take the side of the walk where he can be of most assistance to the lady and allow her the side where the walking is best

A gentleman should always remove his hat entirely when a lady speaks to him on the street—

When he meets a man who has gained eminence or distinction

When he meets a friend who is accompanied by a lady

When asked a question as to direction or for information

When he offers his seat to a lady in a car

When he enters an elevator where a lady is a passenger

A gentleman should go before a lady upstairs and allow her to precede him when coming down

A gentleman should allow a lady to enter a door first. The lady should go before the man, both going into and out of a church or assembly hall

A lady should always bow first

A lady should always acknowledge a favor shown her

A lady does not have to "demand" the consideration of a gentleman and there is no use trying to demand it from one who is not

A gentleman should show his wife as much consideration on the street as he pays to other women

HOME MANNERS

A man should be as gentle at home as when abroad. Because he is at home is no reason why he should be gruff

"Public manners" that are not put to use at home are "put on" and bogus

A woman should be as considerate of her own children's feelings as she is of those of others

There is no reason why the family should not be as polite with their table etiquette when dining by themselves as when they have company

A child should be taught to take off its hat when addressing his parents and when it comes into the room

A child that speaks disrespectfully of its parents will do so to others

A mother or father who rails at their children is sowing seeds of discord in the family that will reap a wild harvest when the child leaves the home place

Your sister is as much entitled to your courtesy as is the sister of any other man

TABLE MANNERS

The fork should be used to put food in the mouth except soups and desserts that are made to eat from a spoon. The knife should never be put in the mouth for any purpose. It is made to cut with and nothing else

In eating from a spoon do not make a "sucking" noise

Teach all children from the very first bite to chew all solid food thoroughly. They do not learn it naturally. To gulp food is neither good for the health nor is it at all nice

A child started right with good table manners will always retain them. Started wrong it is liable never to change

If you wear a mustache, do not "suck" juices or meat from it. It is dangerous to health and very bad manners to do so. Wipe it off

In dining with or without company, any member of the family wishing to be served should say, "Please help me to the ———" When wishing to be excused always ask the housewife (mother or sister or whoever occupies that position) if you may be excused before you arise from the table and remain seated until you get the desired consent

No food should be carried to the mouth with the hands except bread or cake Pie should be eaten with a fork

You must not bend down over your plate in order to get your mouth close to it It would be better even to bring the plate up to the mouth than to do this, still BOTH are wrong Sit erect and bring your food to your mouth with the fork

Do not "shovel" food in the mouth with fork or knife or spoon take what food will make a nice bite by sticking the prongs of the fork into it and carrying it to the mouth

If you cannot eat without your mouth "leaking" you had better go out behind the house and practice until you can

Do not spit food out of your mouth on anything If you have food or a bone or anything in your mouth which you do not want to swallow, hold the fork or spoon up to your mouth and very quietly place it on the fork or spoon and deposit it on a bone dish or on the side of your plate

Do not place any of the refuse of your dinner on the table cloth If you have no side dish or bone dish to put it on, place it on your plate

COMPANY DINNER

For company dinner the order of sitting down at the table is all visiting ladies first, then all visiting gentlemen, then the host and lastly the hostess

If you are not in the habit of saying grace at your own table, be sure to have grace when you have even one visitor who follows that habit, be considerate of the wishes and habits of the least of your guests

In rising from a dining with company, the host should arise first, followed by the gentlemen visiting, then the hostess should arise, followed by the visiting ladies

If you wish to be excused from the table ask the hostess to excuse you before you rise Upon receiving "certainly" as an answer from the one addressed, you may arise and if you wish say "I have certainly enjoyed your nice dinner," or some similar words Then bow and retire Do not linger to talk after you have arisen from the table Be sure you have said all you want to before you ask to be excused

In serving company dinner serve all visiting ladies first, then all gentlemen, then the hostess and then the host, if the host is serving the plates If a waiter is serving the plates then follow the same order except that the host should be served just before the hostess Of course, if the dinner is entirely informal, the diners may be served one side of the table at a time beginning at the farthest from the host

In serving 'course" dinners, the order is soups, fish with relishes meats with relishes, pastries cakes, cheese, nuts, fruits, coffee and cigars This order should be followed whether you have a three-course or a ten-course dinner The above is for an eight-course dinner Unless the bread is to be served hot it should be placed on the table before dinner is announced No other food should be on the table at the beginning of the meal, except nuts and fruits

IN GENERAL

In conversing, never "dispute " It is rude and crude If you conscientiously differ from the one you are conversing with, before you dispute his word ask permission to "differ from" him and then argue the matter with due regard to his feelings and convictions

Do not try to bulldoze another into taking your way of thinking of a matter If he is forced into it without reason he will be of the same opinion still

A fight never did settle a matter Arbitration is always in order

Do not talk family matters to others Do not try to pry into the family matters of others

Never look over another's shoulder when he is writing

Do not "listen in" on a telephone conversation

Do not make the mistake of thinking that it takes courage to fight It takes more courage to keep out of a fight

Might never made right and never will If you are forced to fight for the right be sure you fight right It is better always to avoid a difficulty even at the risk of being called · a coward If you are forced to defend yourself against a bully, fight your best but do not force the fight on him A bully is a "thing" that needs to be avoided

J. Will Jones.

Wm. M. Young.

Wm. Allen.

B. M. Patten.

J. W. Belle.

J. M. Southwell.

A. L. Rutherford.

J. E. McNealy.

A. G. Perkins

Miss Estella B. Jackson

A. G. Perkins, Jr.　　　　Office and Staff of A. G. Perkins & Co.　　　　Bertram Hicks

A G PERKINS

A G Perkins, lawyer and economist, head of A G Perkins & Company, was born in Galveston, Texas He is engaged in the law, land and loan business with offices at Houston and Galveston Texas His grandfather was Alfred Perkins, one of Galveston's earliest settlers after the war and the first of his race to provide for the education of the freedman Alfred Perkins provided the land and aided to built the Barnes Institute at Galveston, Texas, the first school for the education of the African-American and their descendants The father of A G Perkins was the late Geo Perkins, forty-six years a deacon of the oldest Baptist church in Texas and who took much interest in the general uplift and progress of his race The mother of A G Perkins was the late Susan Bird Perkins Their efforts formed the predicate by which the Perkins family has become favorably known The family take their name from a prominent ante and post-bellum white family, who after the war established at Galveston, Texas, A J Perkins & Co, predecessors of Moore & Goodman, lumber dealers and mill owners

A G Perkins, the subject of this sketch, was educated in the public schools of Galveston, being the valedictorian of the first class of graduates of the Central High School, J R Gibson, principal He attended Bishop College, Marshall, Texas For several years he was a teacher in the public schools of Galveston, was United States Inspector of Customs, was connected with the United States Census Department at Galveston in 1900, and the United States Census Department at New York City in 1910, was admitted to the practice of the law in 1900 before the late Judge William H Stewart, Galveston, Texas, who for nearly forty years was judge of the District Court of Galveston County, Texas, was ordained to the ministry in 1905 by Rev A Barbour, Chairman of the Ordination Board, and in the City of New York, where he resided for several years, devoted much of his time to a study of the social industrial and economic conditions of the African-Americans and their descendants, as well as their political and civic status from the legal viewpoint, is general secretary of the Industrial Foundation U S A, an organization devoted to industrial research and development, is a member of many organizations, is general attorney for the Most Worshipful Grand Lodge of Free and Accepted Masons of Texas, Special Deputy Grand Master and Worshipful Master of South Gate Lodge, No 32, F & A M, Galveston, Texas is a member of Grand Chapter of Eastern Star, has attended State and National Republican conventions, and as a property owner ranks second among his people in Galveston. Dr L M Wilkins ranking first

Miss Estella B Jackson, executive manager of the Houston offices of A G Perkins & Co, was born in Columbus, Texas Her grandmother, Mrs Mary Sanders, was among the first and largest property owners of her race in Columbus Julia, the older of Mrs Sanders' two daughters who very early became Mrs Wm Jackson, is the mother of her only girl, Estella B She attended the public school at Columbus and is a graduate of Guadalupe College, Seguin Texas and Mary Allen Seminary, Crockett, Texas Miss Jackson enjoys the distinction of being the first and only notary public of her race and sex in Harris County Her ability is versatile She is an accomplished dressmaker and vocalist Her experience in connection with the law, land and loan business of A G Perkins & Co has given her the opportunity to demonstrate her efficiency and she has proved herself quite equal to her responsibilities

Bertram Hicks, general office assistant for A G Perkins & Co, was born in Houston Texas, about twenty years ago Mr Hicks was educated in the public schools of Houston, Texas, being a graduate of the 1915 class He has been in the employ of A G Perkins & Co over two years Up to the time of his graduation he worked for the firm before and after school hours. He bids fair to become a promising man. He is respectful, gentle and attentive in his conduct. He is one of three children of Mr and Mrs Charles W Hicks who have resided in Houston for many years. Young Hicks devotes his attention to the real estate, rentals and collections of A G Perkins & Co. In addition to this young Hicks is interested in the making and manufacture of floor mops. He has many customers for the Hicks' make and is optimistic that his make some day may be generally used

A G Perkins, Jr, son of A G Perkins (A G Perkins & Co), is the only child in his family. He was born in Galveston, Texas, seventeen years ago. He has attended the public schools of Galveston the public schools of New York City, Houston College, Houston, Texas, and is now a student at Wiley University, Marshall, Texas. Young Perkins from his earliest childhood has always manifested an interest in his father's endeavors, and at a very early age learned to operate a typewriting machine with much aptness and accuracy. After school he devotes himself to assisting in the law, land and loan business of A G Perkins & Co. He is much given to outdoor life, mechanical and electrical investigation and in these lines has already attracted a bit of attention

Mrs. John Adkins.

W. S. Morris.

Gibson Porter.

R. W. Brooks.

E. W. Stokes.

Rev. W. H. Cannon.

M. Hogrobrooks.

J. S. Rutledge.

A. G. Felder. Mrs. A. G. Felder. Mrs. J. A. King.

Mrs. Mary Moore. Mrs. Annie Hagen.

Mrs. M. A. Black. Rev. C. C. Cooper. Mrs. C. C. Cooper.

C. G. HARRIS, "The Camera Man"

The oblique and efficient official photographer of the Houston Red Book will answer calls by wheel and make photos anywhere in Harris or Galveston Counties. Satisfaction guaranteed. 811 San Felipe Street, Houston, Texas. Phone Preston 5960.

NEGRO HEALTH PROBLEM
By Dr. H. E. LEE

As one rises higher and higher in the intellectual, financial and social realms, he gets a clearer conception of human possibilities, he understands more clearly God's purpose in creation; he becomes more appreciative of the things which God has created for his comfort and happiness, and hence feels it a duty to live long upon the earth that God's purposes go not to naught. Realizing this fact, we ask ourselves the question, why should one die out of time? In God's creation there is all that is necessary or essential to a life of three score and ten, and he who dies short of that age does so as a penalty, either direct or indirect, for the violation of one or more of nature's laws.

So much has the subject of the preservation of health and the prolongation of life begun to interest the whole people, that greater activity than has ever before been manifested can be clearly seen by persons in all walks of life.

In the solution of this intricate problem, I am glad to see, late though it may be, that the more fortunate of God's creation from a financial, social and intellectual standpoint are beginning, as never before, to realize that to preserve their own integrity, their own social standing, their own lives, they must lend a helping hand to their unfortunate neighbor. Putting it in a more simple way, I would state that if A would desire to live long, he must interest himself concerning the health conditions surrounding the premises of his neighbor B who unfortunately is unable to change or to have changed the conditions under which he must live. If B is left to himself to become a victim to transmissible diseases, he becomes a common carrier of disease germs and a source of its spread to his neighbor, A.

During the period of slavery, the motive which moved the masters to guard and protect the health of their slaves was prompted by his desire that the earning capacity of each individual slave be kept to the highest possible degree of proficiency. Upon that, more than any other thing, his market value was determined and the real worth as a farm hand depended. Selfish though the motive might have been, yet as a result of that motive the race was preserved through 200 years of servitude, demonstrating that God works out all His plans through the minds of men when ofttimes they are least aware.

With the severance of the chain which bound master to slave, the Negro was thrown out upon his own resources to combat all problems of life known to a struggling people. Ignorant and destitute, he began to work upon the solutions of problems for which he had made no preparations and about which he knew nothing. There were intellectual problems, social problems, financial problems, religious problems and health problems which were his to solve and, like an untrained soldier upon the battlefield, you can imagine how much energy was uselessly expended before he even found the path which led to his much-coveted goal, but which, when found, the hardest fight had just begun I shall not attempt to go into a detailed discussion of the many obstacles with which he was confronted in his efforts at solutions of the social, intellectual, moral and religious problems, but shall attempt to direct my remarks to "The Negro Health Problem "

Since life and health depend so much upon proper housing, wholesome food and sanitation, one can readily see the gravity of the situation regarding the Negro immediately after emancipation and even now, for that matter.

Being unable to construct his own house in which to live, the Negro had to content himself with just such houses as his landlord built and as, with his meagre earnings, he was able to rent These houses, which could be more appropriately called death traps, were built without any regard to ventilation and sanitation In the larger cities can be seen three and four such houses situated upon one lot and in which large families live, sometimes as many as five and six sleeping in one room. To each house upon that lot is a surface closet, the back yards are kept wet from one day to another from wash water, and there is every condition conducive to the origination and the spread of those diseases which develop and thrive under such unsanitary conditions The happy landlord, however, is residing with his family happily and healthfully upon the paved boulevards, having no thought or concern about the helpless poor and the innocent children who are dying in the death traps which he has constructed, knowing at the time their unfitness for human occupancy

These houses are ofttimes occupied by several different families at different times, some of whom may be suffering with such diseases as typhoid fever and tuberculosis Without any effort at fumigation, other families move in in close succession after its having been vacated by the former occupants, only to find, within a short period of time, some member or members of that family having contracted the disease

Right here the City Health Board owe it to the unfortunate poor not only to see that all vacated houses are fumigated before being offered for occupancy to another, but that a general supervision should be had over the construction of every tenant house No permit should be issued for the construction of a house until the lot has been inspected and the lot so well drained as to not permit water to stand under the house after rains Not only that, they should make certain regulations regarding the construction of houses with regard to ventilation and light Until such steps are taken, the high mortality among the tenant class will continue and as a consequence the lives of all the people will be placed in jeopardy in so much as they are thrown in contact with this host of people who expectorate millions of disease germs upon our thoroughfares daily

It seems that our only hope of escape from the above mentioned conditions is home ownership Statistics will bear me out in the assertion that the death rate among those who own their own homes is much lower than that among tenants The average man who is industrious enough to buy a home is likewise industrious enough to see to it that his premises are kept in a healthful condition Too, he and his family are not exposed to the diseases of former occupants That being true, all of us should endeavor to get homes of our own, humble though they may be

So many diseases which are responsible for the high death rate among our people can be traced to cheap and unwholesome foodstuffs Great care should be exercised in the selection of articles of food Only the best should be had and should be bought from the most reliable dealers Decaying vegetables, half spoiled meats, and old can goods are responsible for the death of many of our people

General sanitation is a condition over which we have little or no control Seemingly, by the process of elimination, we find ourselves segregated. As a rule, if there is a low, marshy place in the larger cities where drainage is almost impossible and where malaria, typhoid fever and tuberculosis are constantly present, we are assigned to that region with the promise that when we are once established, the city will extend its sewers and we will be afforded every assistance toward making our locality sanitary and suitable in which to live. Once we are there our petitions are lost off the files and we are forgotten. Not until the development of a case of typhoid or of tuberculosis in the home of the well-to-do can be traced to the servant does there come a realization of the fact that the independent is safe only in so much as the dependent is protected. These germs do not develop in the well-kept homes, but once carried there by the servant even, may find suitable soil for its development and may produce one of the most violent forms of the disease peculiar to its nature. No city or locality is more sanitary than its most unsanitary spot wherever that spot may be.

In the South the Negro is the mainstay upon the farm and, in fact, in all places where hard physical exertion is needed. Hence, every day lost because of illness means not only a loss to himself, but a certain per cent of loss to his employer. Hence, as such, his health should be as well guarded as was it when his master stood on duty.

Based upon the above mentioned facts, the Southern Sociological Congress is doing much to arouse sufficient interest as to changed living conditions among colored people and thereby stamp out those diseases which are preventable. The colored people throughout the South should co-operate with this movement since it means to improve living conditions among our people.

With a diminution in the birth rate and an increase in the death rate, together with practically no increase from immigration, one can readily see that the race is destined to extermination. As a race, we should become more concerned about existing conditions and begin a health campaign of education among our people. From the pulpits, lecture platforms, in the public schools and fraternal organizations, our people should be taught how to preserve their health. Young women should be taught that there is no higher position in life and no place where one can be more highly esteemed than a mother in a home. The future destiny of our race depends very largely upon the mothers of the future generations. When women get a clear conception of the importance of proper motherhood, when they are brought into a realization of the fact that the men who are to bring about the proper solution of the race problem must be the product of the best there is in motherhood, they will not be so inclined to the practice of abortions which is sure and certain to wreck the life of her who practices it.

When men are brought into a realization early in life of the serious effect of venereal diseases upon their offspring, they will refrain from those practices which are calculated to bring about those conditions such as we so often see upon our streets. In this field there is an opportunity for much effective work along the lines of the solution of the health problem among our people.

The crowded conditions of our public schools comes in for consideration in the solution of the health problem, for it is in these places where our children spend from seven to eight hours per day for a period of nine months in the year and covering a period of from twelve to fourteen years. This being the developing period of their lives, makes it the more serious. As a result of the crowded conditions and the wet playgrounds during rainy seasons, development is arrested, especially among the girls, and they leave school to suffer from these effects through life. Parents should interest themselves and organize school improvement clubs and with their own means, if necessary, make those needed improvements that are essential to health and comfort of their children.

If we as a race are to be preserved, much of the work will have to be accomplished by our own efforts. That fact is evident and cannot be denied. Realizing that then, we must bestir ourselves and begin a crusade against those preventable diseases that are destroying our people by the thousands each year. Typhoid fever, tuberculosis and the venereal diseases must be and can be stamped out.

I appeal to you through this article to begin at once with renewed determination to wage a war and to continue the fight until these diseases are extinct and the death rate among our people is reduced from its present figures.

The Western Star Publishing Co., organized in 1895 at Dallas with Rev. E. W. D. Isaac, manager and editor of the then known Baptist Star, a five-column, four-page newspaper, has steadily grown. The firm was transferred to Houston about 1900, having as managers and editors Rev. R. T. Taylor and J. M. Codwell, deceased, and Rev. F. L. Lights. The present manager and managing editor, E. D. Pierson, came into control in September, 1905, finding a mere "junk pile" of wornout out-of-date material and an ink-besmirched sheet of five columns. He had the firm, which was a partnership, incorporated in 1908, and the paper changed to a six-column quarto. The plant has so grown, under his management, that now it is valued at more than $5000 and the paper has been changed to a full size seven-column, eight-page weekly, with over 10,000 circulation. The firm furnishes regular employment to from ten to twelve hands daily. While it is the mouth-piece of Texas Negro Baptists, it is also a general newspaper in line with everything touching race advancement, and is regarded as the cleanest and newsiest newspaper published in the Southwest.

ꜗ | Professional and-Industrial List | ꜗ

Allen, Wm.—1887; Railway Postal Clerk, Class 4; 2218 Stevens Street; native of Louisiana; came to Houston 1908; connected with the postal service for six years. Member of National Alliance of Postal Employees.

Ballard, W. W.—1821 Whitty Street; Superintendent Sloan Memorial Church Sunday School; Secretary Solomon Lodge No. 18, U. B. F.

Bland, A. T.—1879; Porter, 1603 Rusk Street; came to Houston in 1905; formerly employed in oil mill work, but for 13 years has been a porter. He has accumulated several small farm plots and four houses and lots in Richmond, Texas. Master in Masonic Lodge and Past C. C. in K. P.

Beverly, S. B.—Merchant, 2420 McKinney Avenue; phone Preston 6651; been in fish, grocery and meal business for six years. Member of St. John Baptist Church.

Belle, J. W.—1877; Railway Postal Clerk, grade 6; 3314 Stonewall Street; phone Preston 6354. Mr. Belle has one of the nicest cottage homes in the city and an interesting family. He has been in the postal service for six years. Received a Grammar School education. Member Mt. Zion Baptist Church, Smithsonian Lodge No. 155, Masons, and past Secretary of same, and member of the National Alliance of Postal Employees.

Bonner, Rev. O. L.—1865; Minister, 1615 Hill Street; native of Alabama. He began teaching school at the age of fifteen, at the age of sixteen he was converted and felt the call to preach the gospel. He taught school and served as local preacher for nine years, since which time until the present he has devoted his life to the ministry. He joined the Alabama Conference in 1889 and joined the Texas Conference in 1891. This is his thirty-fourth year in the ministry.

Booker, J. G.—1868; Lumber Checker, 1002 Meadow Street; phone Preston 8977; born in Brazoria County and came to Houston in 1900. Owns homestead. Member, Deacon and Sunday School Superintendent of Mt. Zion Baptist Church; G. U. O. of O. F., M. of F. in K. of P.

Branks, R. W.—1859; Transfer Line, 3403 Prince Street; phone Hadley 2746; native of Kentucky; came to Houston in 1906. Member Fourth Missionary Baptist Church, of K. of P., A. O. O. P. Married Miss Fannie Lewis in 1906.

Brown, T. R.—1879; Railway Postal Clerk, grade 4; 2412 Dowling Street; phone Hadley 3407; born in Lavaca County, Texas; came to Houston in 1906. Married in 1902 to Miss B. Nelson. Member and Trustee of St. John's Baptist Church, of National Alliance of Postal Employees, A. O. O. P.; former teacher in business college for 11 years; six years postal clerk.

Burton, Harris—1883; Merchant, 3020 McGowen Street; phone Hadley 2723; born in Richmond, Texas; came to Houston 1897; public school education. Married Miss Irene Thompson in 1909. In mercantile business five years. Owns two-story building at 3020

McGowen Street and five lots Member St John's Baptist Church Deacon and Treasurer of same, K of P and Texas Negro Fair and Park Board

Calhoun, Daniel D —1875, Merchant, 624 Allston, Houston Heights, phone Taylor 1484, born in Marlin, Texas, came to Houston in 1906, graduate Marlin public schools Owns nice home and three rent houses   Member of Damascus Baptist Church, member of Masons, A F & A M, Past Chancellor K of P, I O O M B

Cannon, Rev W H —1875, Minister, residence, Harrisburg Road, phone Preston 6517, native of Louisiana, graduate of New Orleans University, came to Houston 1904 pastor St Mark's Baptist Church and Pleasant Hill Baptist Church   Member of Order of Love and Charity Married Miss Evalyn Simpson 1914   Owns homestead in Louisiana

Carter, J H —1876, Carpenter and Contractor, 1102 Schwartz Street, phone Preston 7938 Member and Sunday School teacher in Baptist Church, of G U. O. O F No 7776

Cebron, Sam—1884 Porter, 3020 Nance Street   Member of Sloan Memorial Church, of G U O O F and U B F Porter for ten years Married twelve years, four children

Cooper, Rev C C.—1877, Minister, 600 Heiner Street, phone Preston 6050, came to Houston 1905; graduate of Houston College   Member of K of P and A M C, President of Council No 5, Board member of Lincoln Southern Association, preaching eight years, Missionary two years Married to Miss Roxie Sherman in 1900

Codwell, Prof J M (deceased)—1865, late residence, 1218 O Neil Street, born in Navasota, Texas, came to Houston in 1900, married to Miss Pearl Cooper of Terrell, Texas, in 1902, two children, Jennie Marie and John Elihu   Member of Antioch Baptist Church and editor Western Star at time of death on August 4, 1914
Prof. Codwell had been prominently connected with the advance movements of his race for many years at the time of his death, and in his death his race lost one of its foremost thinkers and most active workers He was Educational Agent and Secretary of the State Missionary and Educational Convention and Secretary of State Sunday School Convention and member of U B F During his residence in Navasota he was member and deacon of the Baptist Church there and prominently known in educational circles He served on the aldermanic board of the town and was a member of the Grimes County Educational Board, a distinction rarely acquired in Texas He was known throughout his life as an earnest, honest, consecrated Christian man and one whose integrity and veracity was beyond question He deported himself well in all circles and was held in high esteem by all who knew him of both races He enjoyed the supreme confidence of all with whom he came in intimate contact and his record stands as an inspiration to those who know of him in any way He was Assistant Secretary of the National Baptist Convention, and as such, as in all his editorial, teaching, lecturing and administrative work, did valiant service for his people He received his degree at Tillotson College

Covington, Dr B Jessie—1875, Physician and Surgeon, residence, 2219 Dowling Street, phone Hadley 886, office 409½ Milam Street, phone Preston 6436, born in Marlin, Texas came to Houston in 1903 B S of Hearne College in 1892 M D of Meharry Medical College, Nashville, Tenn, 1900 Medical practice 15 years Married in 1902 to Miss Jennie Belle Murphy, one child, Ernestine Jessie Member Bethel Baptist Church, Trustee in same, G U O O F, Masons, U B F, K of P and A O O P

Davenport, T C —1869, Cai Checker, 1311 Arnold Street, phone Hadley 1851, born in Polk County Texas, came to Houston in 1874, employed by F W Heitmann Co for 22 years, now car checker Owns homestead Past Superintendent Sunday School and member of Trinity M E Church, President Trustee Board of same, member Magnolia Lodge A F & A M , Grand Deputy High Priest Royal Arch Masons of Texas, U B F , Past Worthy Shepherd of A O O P

DeGaultie, Harry C —Superintendent of First Texas State Insurance Company, Houston office, born in 1868 at Houston and received education in Houston High School Present office address, 711½ Prairie Avenue, phone Preston 5546, residence, 604 Andrews Street Member and Trustee of Brown's A M E Church, Past Chancellor Knight of Pythias Lodge No 135; Past Supreme Shepherd of Ancient Order of Pilgrims, Ex-Secretary Endowment Board, and Past Grand Superior of Brothers and Sisters of

Love and Charity, Vice-President and Director of Colored Industrial Exposition and Carnival Association, member of Knights and Daughters of Tabor Mr DeGaultie enjoys the supreme confidence of the managing office and his associates

Dickson, Winston M C —Attorney-at-Law, office 409½ Milam Street, phone Preston 1459, born at Crockett, Texas, and came to Houston in 1896 Graduate of Tillotson College 1894, Pomana College 1904, Boston University 1909 Holds A B from Pomana College and J B & J M from Boston University Owns homestead Member of Christian Church

Dixon, M E —1879 Collector, 804 Heiner Street born in Robertson County, Texas, collector for Jackson Undertaking Company Member of Friendship Baptist Church, Deputy Grand Mentor C E W Day Temple

Dickens, W M —1875, 2905 Shepherd Street, native of North Carolina, came to Houston in 1902 Married Miss S E Henderson of Anderson, Texas, in 1907 Owns a nice home Deacon of St John's Baptist Church, Treasurer of Sunday School class

Durham, Dr E A —1865, Physician, residence, 2906 Nance Street, phone Preston 4697, office, 411½ Travis Street, phone Preston 5039, native of Georgia Married Miss Sophronia J Carr in 1885 Came to Houston in 1908 Graduate of Wiley University, Marshall, Texas, 1890, Bennett Electro-Medical College Chicago, Illinois, in 1886 Taught schools seven years Practiced medicine one year at Rush, Texas, 15 years at Calvert, Texas Member of Mt Vernon M E Church

Franklin, Henry—1843, Head Porter Union National Bank, 1602 Jackson Street, native State of Louisiana, came to Houston in 1865 Married Miss Nancy Foster in 1874 Has one boy and seven girls living Member and Trustee Trinity M E Church, and a class leader of same Has been running a transfer line for 30 years and has been connected with the Union National Bank for ten years

Felder. A G —1867, Ice and Fuel, 1605 Andrews Street; phone Preston 7950, born in Washington County, came to Houston in 1897 Member Antioch Baptist Church Married in 1908 Owns homestead Treasurer of K P and G U O O F and Worthy Master of U B F

Garrett, Dr O C, A B—Physician and Surgeon, 417 Robin Street, phone Preston 8149 Graduate of Fisk University 1891, and Meharry Medical College 1904 Ex-Principal of Wesley Graded High School

Gilmore, Benj J—1879, 2202 Stewart Street, phone Hadley 2172, native of South Carolina Married Miss Lillie Patterson of Victoria, Texas, in 1905 Came to Houston in 1902 Member Trinity M E. Church, Steward and class leader, Smithsonian Lodge No 155, Masons Owns nice home

Gilmore, James I—Was born in Mobile, Ala, February 1st, 1860 He is the youngest child of Isaac and Mary Gilmore, who were formerly slaves He is a self-made man His father died when he was not quite seven years of age, leaving his mother a widow with an only child, Jimmie, as he was called by his mother In October, 1870, this boy and his mother came to Texas, landing in Galveston, their future home At the age of 11 years Jimmie was a student of the Blue College, Mobile, Ala during the days of Prof Squires Prof Squires was afterward appointed assistant postmaster of the Mobile postoffice Little James attended the public schools of Galveston having for his teachers the lamented Virginia Patterson (nee Ashe) and Prof Joseph Cuney, now attorney at law He married early in life to Miss Harriett Bowers of Galveston and has been happy in this union for 36 years He professed a hope in Christ in 1881 and united with St Paul's Methodist Episcopal Church He served his home church in the following capacities Steward, Class Leader, Sunday School Superintendent, Secretary of the Board of Trustees, President of the Epworth League, District Epworth League President and represented his district at the first International Epworth League Convention at Cleveland Ohio, in 1893 Recognizing the call to preach, he answered and joined the Texas Conference in December, 1896, at Galveston, Texas, and was appointed to a mission charge. Mallalieu, Houston Texas So acceptably did he serve this work that he was promoted the next year and his promotions were continuous until he was appointed Presiding Elder of the Paris District in December, 1906 He served this district his full term of six years and placed it in the fore rank of the Conference On retiring from the district he was appointed to the pastorate of Mt Vernon Methodist Episcopal Church, Houston, Texas, in November, 1912 He is now serving his fourth year in this same charge having been reappointed each year to succeed himself The Lord has blessed his work in the church and he is counted a successful minister of the gospel He served his Conference for six years as Assistant Treasurer and is now serving as Treasurer for the third year

He is also a favorite in the realm of fraternal societies, being a member of the U B of F, Masons, G U O O F, A O of P K of P, Eastern Star, Mosaic Templars of America, Household of Ruth and Knights and Daughters of Tabor He has served the foregoing institutions both locally and in the Grand bodies He is also Past National Grand Chaplain of the United Brothers of Friendship and Sisters of Mysterious Ten He is one of the seven men who organized and chartered the only Negro fire insurance company in the United States and enjoys the honor of being secretary of the same, the Standard American Mutual Fire Insurance Company of Texas

He is a tireless worker, a lover of his race, a humanitarian, high churchman and a friend of men, being charitable to a fault

Glenn, J G—1874, Mechanical Engineer at I. & G N Shops, 1110 George Street. Member Baptist Church and K P

Goodman, E W—1877, Postal Mail Clerk, 5th grade, 2723 Nance Street, born in Austin County, Texas, came to Houston in 1914   Attended Prairie View Normal three years   Owns homestead in Beaumont   Married Miss Virginia Brown in 1904   Issue, three children, one living   Member of Masons, K P and Woodman Camp

Goodwin Dan G—1871, Merchant, 706 Paige Street, born in Brazoria County, Texas   Member and Deacon Fourth Missionary Baptist Church, Trustee Pride of Houston Lodge No 211, K P, Chief Mentor Fisher Temple No 105, K & D of T and I L A   Owns home and other lots in city

Harmon, J H—Merchant, residence, 1012 Meyer Street, store, 423 San Felipe Street, native of Alabama, came to Houston in 1894   Owns homestead and several other lots in city   Member Bethel Baptist Church and G U O O F, Treasurer of his local and Treasurer of the joint Trustee Board   Graduate of Houston Academy   Dry Goods merchant   Mr Harmon is one of the self-made men of his race in Houston as he was left a double orphan at the age of 13, with nothing to start out in life

Harmon, Master J H Jr—1906 Student, 1012 Meyer Street   Little son of Mr and Mrs J H Harmon   Member Bethel Baptist Church   In fifth grade in public school and third grade in music   Has splendid natural oratorical ability, studious and is religiously inclined

Harper, Columbus C—Pastor of Bethel Baptist Church   Was born in 1884 and began preaching at nine years of age   In 1902 he began pastoring, holding some prominent charges, among which were Mt Olive, Dayton, Ohio, St James Texarkana, Ark, Bethesda, Marshall, Texas and Bethel, of Houston, Texas   He is now retiring to accept the pulpit of St John's Church, Dallas, Texas   Alumnus of Homer Normal College, Burton College and Ohio Central University.

Harris, C G—1873, Photographer, native of Arkansas, came to Houston in 1910 after a successful work of nine years with his photographic studio in Little Rock   He is now the leading Afro-American photographer of the city. He was married to Miss C. L Williams in 1914   Member of Antioch Baptist Church   Has property in Arkansas and Texas

Hayward, James A—1889, Cleaning and Pressing, 2303 McKinney Avenue, phone Preston 1930, born Gladstone, Texas, came to Houston in 1902   Graduate of Houston Public School   Member of the Board of Trustees of Fourth Missionary Baptist Church, Secretary B Y P U and Secretary U B F Lodge

Henry, John—1887, Cleaner and Presser, residence, 1108 Schwartz Street establishment, 2803 Odin Avenue, native State of Texas, came to Houston in 1913   Owns homestead and rent houses   Common school education   Member G U O O F

Henry, Wm McKinley—3018 Austin Street   Member of Mt Zion Baptist Church, Recorder of A O of P   President of Silver Seal Band

Hester, Alexander Z—1865, Cotton Sampler, 1703 West Street, phone Preston 5966, native of Georgia; came to Houston in 1893   Connected with Weld-Neville, Inman Co, Alexander Echols and other prominent cotton firms for 26 years   Member of Wesley Chapel Methodist Church, A F & A M, Past Worshipful Master, Past Secretary and Treasurer

Hill, Rev W. Deams, B D—1866. Baptist Minister, 512 Robin Street, native of Georgia   Educated in High School of Eufaula, Ala, Prairie View Normal and Bishop College, Marshall, Texas   At Bishop College he was made night monitor for the campus   Was received into the Baptist Church in 1882 and began his ministerial work in 1891   Was ordained in Denison the following year   Married to Miss Louisa Ward of Galveston in 1896   They have had three children, one living only a few hours and the other two now living, Wilberforce E D Hill and Precious Ruth Hill   Member Mt Rose Baptist Church, Bastrop   Taught school for 15 years, also taught instrumental and vocal music   Served as principal of the Honey Grove Public High School.   Has pastored the following churches   St Paul, Crockett, Texas, Little Zion, Hillsboro, Texas, Morning Chapel. Sulphur Springs, Texas, Sixth Avenue, Corsicana, Texas, North Eighth Street Waco, Texas, Mt Pleasant, Montgomery, Texas, Mt Rose, Bastrop, Texas, and Beren at Jackson, Tenn   Was a member of the State B Y P U Board for years, is First Vice-President of the State Foreign Mission Convention and Recording Secretary of the State Associated Charities   K of P and Mason

Hagen, Green—1862, Core Maker, 1710 Andrews Street, born in Fort Bend County   Came to Houston in 1865   Public school education   Owns house and two lots in Independence Heights   Member Friendship Baptist Church, Sunday School Superintendent, P D M of U B F

Hogrobrooks, M —1881, Merchant, 2121 Nassau Street, phone Taylor 103, native of Georgia   Has been in the grocery business for nine years and is now member of the firm of Horn & Sons   Member of Second Baptist Church, Houston Heights, Secretary of the Moore Bros Lodge of Christian Union   Married, has two children

Hogrobrooks, Theodore—1885, Mechanic residence West Nineteenth Street, Houston Heights, native of Georgia   Came to Houston in 1900   Member of Second Baptist Church, Houston Heights, member Solomon Temple, L O O M B, No 1   Boss carder at Oriental Textile Mills has been for eight years   Wife, Inez Hogrobrook, born in Houston in 1887   Son. Theodore, Jr, born in Houston in 1912

Holden, Prof P H, B S —Teacher, Head High School History Department, residence, 2917 Turner Street, phone Hadley 2192   Native of Mississippi   Came to Houston in 1907   Graduate of Alcorn A & M College of Mississippi 1905   Present position. Instructor of History   Owns homestead and vacant lots   Member Trinity M E Church, Treasurer of Theola Sanctuary No 301, A O O P

Hunter, Rev W Q —1877 Minister, 917 Saulnier Street, phone Preston 6375, born in Bryan, Texas   Married in 1900   Came to Houston in 1914   Graduate of Borham High School   Owns three houses and lots in Bonham, Texas   Member C M E Church   Ordained in 1913 at Henderson by Bishop M F Jamison   Pastored St Luke C M E Church at Jefferson, Texas   Also member of G U O O F and K of T

Jones, J Will—1867, Railway Postal Clerk, 215 Robin Street, phone Preston 9358, native of Houston   Attended Allen University   Took special course in music at Boston, Mass   Was Director of Music in Wiley University for five years   Member and pipe organist for Trinity M E Church, R W P C 16 years   H of P and N A P E   Married Miss Margarette Morrow in 1897

Jackson, Joseph H —Contractor and Builder   Born at Sandy Point Texas, in 1868   Came to Houston in 1870   Married Miss Lillie C Williams in 1889   Built Trinity M E Church, flats and numerous buildings in Houston   Employs from twelve to fifteen men   Owns four lots at Fidelity

Johnson, A J —1883, Contractor, 319 Robin Street, phone Preston 6151   Member Wesley Chapel A M E Church, U B F and A O O P   Graduate of High School and Los Angeles Architectural School   Has been contractor and builder for eight years during which time he has built many of the nice homes of the city for his race   His reputation is such that when the contract is given him, those having the work done know that it will be done right and the best possible way

Johnson, James A —1845, Teamster, 1847 W 17th Street, phone Taylor 1351, native of Georgia   Married Miss Georgia Hunt in 1871   Came to Texas in 1864   Member Second Baptist Church   Owns home and other property

Kyle James—1846   Superintendent Olivewood Cemetery, 520 Hopson Street, phone Preston 6784, native of Brazoria County, Texas   Owns homestead   Trustee of Trinity M E Church, A R & A M and W O of P   Married in 1869

Lockett, Prof Richard G , A B —1882, Teacher, 1901 Worms Street, phone Preston 9126, native of Houston   Graduate of Atlanta University 1905   Teacher in High School, Houston   Owns homestead and other property   Trustee Mt Vernon M E Church   One of the Supreme Trustees of A O O P   Trustee and one of the founders of Carnegie Colored Library at Houston

Longcope, Ed L —1882, Contractor and Builder, 3004 Market Street, phone Preston 8942

Luckey, Will—Yardman, 3102 Turner Street; native of Lewis, Texas   Married Miss Mary Marshall of Edna, Texas, in 1904   One child   Came to Houston in 1894   Member St James Baptist Church, U B of F and A M B A

Lumpkin, Wm —1018 Andrews Street, member Masonic, A O O P and only Afro-American in Houston member of Bricklayers' International Union

McClellan, George—Of Beverly & McClellan, 2420 McKinney Avenue, phone Pr 6651

McCoy, Bailey —1875   Salesman, 1505 Pannell Street, phone Preston 1210, native of Grimes County, Texas, came to Houston in 1892   Employed by Heitmann Company since 1900   Married Miss L Miller in 1913   Owns homestead   Member Trinity M E Church and K of P

McCullough, P H —1880, with Brown Cracker & Candy Company, owns homestead   Married Miss O B McCloncy in 1906   Choir member of Bethel Baptist Church   President of Magnolia Dramatic Club   High School education

McMillan, D B —1887, Parcel Post Carrier, 2210 Gray Avenue, phone Hadley 2657, native of Bryan, Texas   Married Miss Zelma C Graves of Richmond, Texas   Two children, Daniel B and Nolan M   Came to Houston in 1909   Graduate of Prairie View Normal in 1907   Owns a nice home and other property   Member Dunbar No 304, A O O P

McMurray. Albert—1871, 3602 Fulton Street. native of Columbus, Texas Came to Houston in 1875 Graduate of Houston High School 1885 Trustee of St John's Baptist Church, Treasurer of choir Member Negro Y M C A, A O O P Owns two-story store building on Fulton and Wall Streets besides residence and other property

McKinney, Van H—411½ Travis Street, is the pioneer Negro job printer of Texas His office was established in 1892 in the City of Houston Since that time a score of colored boys have learned the printer's trade under him and are today out in the world doing well, namely Mr W O Myers and Van R McKinney, present employees, Campbell A Gilmore of Gilmore & Lethridge Co, this city, Jacob Leake, editor and proprietor of the Palestine Hustler, Palestine, Texas, Will Hamilton holds a position in the government printing office, Washington, D C W L Jones, former editor and proprietor of the Galveston-Houston Times, at present postmaster at Boley, Okla, Will Mayo, who holds a lucrative position in a white office in Louisiana, Charles H Cornell, J B Fenley (deceased). W O. Wilson and others Mr McKinney is editor of the Houston Van, published weekly in the interest of the business social, religious and moral life of the Negro race

Miller, Prof W E—1871, Teacher. 310 Robin Street, phone Preston 2762, native of Belton, Bell County, Texas Married Miss Ida O Levy May 2, 1894 Came to Houston in 1892 Graduate of Prairie View College 1890 Owns very nice home Secretary Antioch Baptist Church, member Masonic, K of P, U B of F, A O of P, Secretary Old Land Mark Baptist Association, Secretary Mason Lodge fourteen consecutive years

Mitchell, Henry J—1874, Hotel Waiter, 1901 Pannell Street phone Preston 4676, native of Houston Owns home and other property in Harris County Married Miss Frankie J Johnson in 1898 Trustee St Paul A M E Church, P C C of K of P Junior Warden Masons, President H M B A, Ex-Secretary G U O O F, Past Secretary U B F, K of T, and Trustee Texas Negro Fair Association

Monroe, W H—1865, Requisition Clerk Guarantee Life Insurance Co, 2502 Gray Avenue, phone Hadley 3242, native of Missouri Came to Houston in 1896 Educated in public schools of Kansas City Formerly barber For eight years in the above position, which he has filled to the satisfaction of all He has a large circle of friends both among the white and colored of Houston Owns home Member Antioch Baptist Church, S W of Masons Prelate of K of P Married Miss Mamie L Tanner of Brenham in 1898 Has interesting family of five boys and three girls, who are receiving the right kind of training to make them useful citizens

Morris, W S—1879; Proprietor Barber Shop, 2515 McKinney Avenue. native of Texas, came to Houston in 1908 Member Mt Calvary Baptist Church, U B F. A F and A M and A O O P

Moore, G A—202 Andrews Street Prominent church worker Treasurer of G U O O F, K & D of T

McNealy, J E—1876, Railway Postal Clerk, 1707 West Street, native of Texas, came to Houston in 1902 In the postal service as Mail Clerk for over nine years Member of Mt Zion Baptist Church, K P A F & A M Has High School education and owns home and other property in Houston

Mosely, Rev James L—1872, Edwards Street phone Preston 6954 Married Miss Lillie R Twiggs in 1907 Five children Educated in public schools Taught school for 21 years Conducted several summer normals Ordained in 1907 Pastored at Victoria Columbus, Sealy, Chappell Hill Now pastor of St Paul M E Church Member Masons and Texas Conference

Noble, C H—1864, Harrisburg native of Houston   Graduate of Reagan High School of Houston Married Mrs Ruby Nevels in 1905 Owns home and store Member Antioch Baptist Church, Prelate in K P, and Grand Chaplain H M B A For 24 years a professional cook

Nowlin, Rev S S—Minister, 2409 Lamar Avenue Member Fourth Missionary Baptist Church, I O of 12 and U K and L of H

Nelson, S M—1879, Contractor, 2409 Hadley Avenue; phone Hadley 321, native of Victoria, Texas Came to Houston in 1903 Graduate of Wylie University 1903 Owns home and other property in Houston Member Trinity M E Church and class leader, K P and A O O P Married Miss Viola L Evander in 1905 Two children

Paley, Adam D—1878, Stock Keeper Southwestern Paper Co, 1310 George Street, native of Waller County, Texas Came to Houston in 1899 Graduate of public school in 1896 Owns farm near Berkshire Texas Deacon Bethel Baptist Church K P

Patten, Mason B—1871, Railway Postal Clerk, 1018 Ruthven Street, phone Preston 6243 Graduate of Prairie View Normal 1896 Owns home and other property in Houston and San Antonio Formerly principal of Huntsville public school for 14 years Member Wesley Chapel A M E Church M B O & R M A Ry, N A P E; Associate Editor N A P E, President Postal Inv Association Married Miss Pauline B Garza in 1899

Phillips, Frank—802 San Felipe Street, phone Preston 5684 Realty and property owner Member G U O O F, Masonic, Trustee and Treasurer Fourth Baptist Church

Polk, Jos W—1889 Shipping Clerk, 1404 Bayou Street, native of Houston Member of Mt Vernon M E Church, G U O O F

Porter, G—1874, Cleaning and Pressing, 2313 Dowling Street, native of Louisiana Married Miss Ella N Gidry in 1893 One child, Joseph Porter Came to Houston in 1913 Member St John's Baptist Church, Masonic Property in Louisiana

Porter, Rev H P—He was born March 15th, 1879, in Rusk County, Texas Joined the C M E Church when 8 years old Attended the public schools until 15 years old, at which time he entered Texas College, working morning and evening for white people to pay his expenses He remained here for six years, finishing college preparatory He was licensed to preach at the age of 16, but being in school and teaching several years after coming out of school, he did not join the Conference as a regular pastor until 1905 under Bishop C H Phillips, A M, M D, D D (East Texas) C M E Church He has served as pastor of some of the best churches of his denomination At this date he is Presiding Elder of the Houston District, member of the General Educational Board of his church for two years Editor of the Southwestern Index Was delegate to the general conference of his church in St Louis in 1914 He is the son of good Christian parents (Mr and Mrs Geo Porter) He married Miss Elnora Brox (Porter) in November, 1902 One little daughter (Bernice Porter) was born to them December 22, 1903

Rankin, Rev D H —Baptist Minister, 800 Crosby Street, phone Preston 9364, pastor Damascus Missionary Baptist Church, Moderator of the Independent Missionary Baptist Association of Texas and Moderator of the La Grange Western Landmark Association, Vice-President of the Baptist State Convention, member of National Baptist Publishing Board of National Baptist Convention Twenty-seven years of his life has been given to ministerial work and to the moral, social and educational uplift of his people The last twenty years of his life have been spent with two congregations

Rhodes, Rev W H —1870, Minister, native of Galveston Came to Houston when a boy Graduate of public schools Married Miss Minnie Barcley in 1907 Issue, two children, Stella Howard and Ernest Rhodes Pastor New Mt Pilgrim Baptist Church Has been in the ministry for nine years

Robinson, Edward W —1881, Railway Postal Clerk, 1802 Dowling Street, phone Hadley 3803 Graduate of Prairie View Normal 1904 Member Antioch Baptist Church. K P In railway postal service for nine years, class 4 Married Miss Gertrude Jeter in 1906, who was born at Beaumont in 1887 and graduate of public high school Owns nice two-story residence Native Orange, Texas Came to Houston in 1909

Robinson, James—1861, native Austin Came to Houston in 1890 Member A M E Church, Sunday School and class leader

Robinson, Rev Jno —1876, Pastor Gallilee Missionary Baptist Church Native of Taylor County, Texas Came to Houston in 1895 Graduate of La Grange High School Ordained in Houston Member S W C B and U B F

Robinson, R C —1882, Porter, 3310 Hadley, phone Hadley 737 Native of Cuero, Texas Came to Houston in 1905 Member K of P

Robinson, W —1878, 613 Robin Street; phone Preston 8165 Native of Louisiana Came to Houston in 1910 Married in 1905 Member Bethel Baptist Church and Masons

Robinson, C R —1875, Barber, 620 Allston Street, Houston Heights native of Georgia Came to Houston in 1896 Owns store with hall and barber shop Member of Antioch Baptist Church, Deputy G M of I O of M B Has rent houses and amusement park

Russell, J G —1861, S Engineer, 1707 Velasco Street Attended public school Steward Fourth M E Church, P M. Mason Married Miss Cora Wallace in 1914

Rutherford, A L —1877, Railway Mail Clerk, 1802 Fowler Street, phone Taylor 2465 Native of Freestone County, Texas Came to Houston in 1912 Married Miss Jennie McGregor in 1893 Former occupation, farmer and teacher for twelve years in public schools Owns home in Houston and property in Marlin, Texas Member St Paul A M E Church, N A P E

Rutledge, James S —1876, Railway Postal Clerk 11 years, class 6, 1208 Crockett Street, phone Preston 5215 Native of Hempstead, Texas Came to Houston in 1904 Deacon and Trustee New Hope Baptist Church A F & A M, N A P E Married Miss Mollie Moore in 1906 Three children

Sanderson, Prof J C—Teacher, Assistant Principal Bruce School   Member A O O P, Masonic and K P

Scott, W M—1853, Hotel Waiter, 715 Ruthven Street, native of Richmond, Va Owns homestead   Married to Miss Eliza Bates in 1897   Have one adopted child   Member of Friendship Baptist Church, G U O O F

Simpson, S J—1884, Merchant, 1302 San Felipe Street, phone Preston 9834 Native of Texas   Came to Houston in 1910   Formerly employed with Pullman Company   Married Miss Emma Shelton in 1906   Owns three lots and four rent houses Member Mt Zion Baptist Church, K. P   Proprietor grocery and all day meat market

Smith, Ernest Olington—The subject of this sketch is a type of the energetic, clean, intelligent young giants that Fisk University and such schools are sending out   He was born at Shelby, Ala, July 4, 1880   He was educated in the elementary schools of Birmingham Ala, and later at Fisk University at Nashville, Tenn, from which school he received the degree of B A   He is at present principal of the Booker T Washington School and the B K Bruce public night school, having been the principal of the first night school established for colored people, and the first person in the Houston school system to hold two positions at the same time   He finds time to be superintendent of a Sunday School, a deacon of the church, a member of the Knights of Harmony and president of the colored Carnegie Library, which was organized by him

Southwell, J M—1890, Railway Postal Clerk   Native of Jasper County, Texas Came to Houston in 1911   High school graduate   Railway postal clerk three years, class 2   Member Missionary Baptist Church, N A P. E, Houston Local   Began teaching public school at the age of fifteen   Taught five years   On postal examinations made more than 99 per cent

Stafford, John Thomas—2518 Mills Street   Native of Ohio and educated in Oberlin Taught school 42 years in the States of Ohio, Missouri and Texas   Married in Weston, Mo, in 1871   Issue seven boys and two girls   Member A M E Church, as is also his wife

Stokes, Frank W—Born in Bellville, Texas, in 1884   Came to Houston in 1902 Married Mrs Mattie Graham in 1906   Owns oil lots, etc   Member and steward Wesley Chapel A M E Church   Secretary City of Refuge Lodge No 287, Masons, and W S of Lily of the Valley, A O O P

Taylor, Burt F, & Co—Manufacturing Jewelers and Opticians, phone Preston 2686   Complicated watch repairing a specialty   311 San Felipe Street   The only complete jewelry establishment owned and run by colored people in the South

Tate, Prof Charles C—1857, Teacher, 1820 St Emanuel Street   Native of Alabama Graduate Bishop College   Teaching 30 years   Owns home and forty-acre farm   Married Johanna Goolsby in 1895   Wife member of Antioch Baptist Church, K & D of T and L O T

Thomas, Linn—1872 Merchant, residence 1618 Capron Street   Established business in 1912 at 902 Schwartz Street   Member Shiloh Baptist Church, U B F

Washington, L—1851, Transfer Line and Landlord, 3006 Nance Street, phone Preston 7118 Native of Texas Came to Houston in 1888 Member of Mt Zion Baptist Church, K P and G U O O F

Watkins, Prof P H—Teacher, 1108 Andrews Street Mason

Williams, Henry N—1902, Student, 1407 San Felipe Street Member of Friendship Baptist Church

Williams, James—1867, Porter, 3519 Broadway Street Native of Tennessee Married Miss Olive Miller in 1895 Came to Houston in 1894 Trustee St John's Baptist Church, Secretary of Rose of Sharon No 12, A O O P , Secretary Pilgrim's Hall Board Trustees South Gate Lodge No 195, U B F

Williams, Julius W—1871, Coffee Roaster 9 years, 1407 San Felipe Street Native of Houston Graduate High School Married in 1908 Member of Friendship Baptist Church, Deacon and Sunday School Teacher One lot in Sunny Side

Young, Wm —1871, Railway Postal Clerk, 2719 Rice Street Native of Victoria, Texas Has been in postal service 14 years President Board of Trustees of Calvary M E Church, Houston Local N A P E , Treasurer Postal Investment Association, A O O. P Married Miss Leonora Lott in 1895

Classified Business, Professional and Industrial List of Afro-Americans in Houston, Revised to May 1, 1915

A Glance at This List Will Put You in Touch With the One You Want in Every Line of Activity.   Classified as to Business Alphabetically.

ATTORNEYS-AT-LAW.

Broyles, M. Hannon ... 714½ Prairie Avenue
Burgess, G. O. ... Courtland and 36th Avenue, Independence Heights
Dickson, W. M. C. ... 409½ Milam Street, Phone Preston 1459
Millard, Oscar C. ... 411½ Travis Street, Phone Preston 5039
Lewis, J. V. ... 1218 Wilson Street, Phone Preston 6076
Lewis, M. G. ... 714½ Prairie Avenue
Perkins, A. G. ... 418½ Travis Street

BARBERS AND BARBER SHOPS.

Barton, Jackson ... 1210 Paige Street
Barton, Ripley ... 2314 Congress Avenue
Bolden, Albert ... 2610 Scott Street
Bush, James ... 1005 San Felipe Street
Byers, Aaron ... 506 Milam Street
Chester, W. W. ... Basement Stewart Building, Phone Preston 3274
Chumley & Scott ... 1017 Prairie Avenue
Clark, Frank ... 408 Milam Street
Clay, Frank ... 3301½ Cline Street
Cornish, J. F. ... 3003 Nance Street
Gray, F. J. ... 908 Franklin Avenue, Preston 9080
Guyden, A. D. ... 85 Marsh Street
Hall, E. H. ... 419 Milam Street
Haller, J. J. ... 2817 Dowling Street
Harrison, L. V. ... 409 Milam Street
Howard & Coleman ... 811 Washington Avenue
Jenkins, Robert ... 2414 McKinney Avenue, Preston 9420
Jorden, Wm. ... 3118 Dallas Street
Leak, Robert ... 2806 Washington Avenue
Logan, Joe ... 507 San Felipe Street, Preston 2413
McKinney, James ... 2016 Congress Avenue
Merida, J. J. ... 906 Prairie Avenue
Mills, James ... 704 Paige Street
Moore, F. M. ... 807 W. 8th Avenue, Houston Heights
Morgan, B. M. ... 517 San Felipe Street
Morris, W. S. ... 2515 McKinney Avenue
Ogden Barber Shop ... 413 Milam Street
Perry, Henry ... 2720 Odin Avenue
Price, J. H. ... 92 Gable Street
Robertson, Frank ... 68 Schrimpf Street
Robinson, C. R. ... 624 Allston Street, Houston Heights
Robinson, J. E. ... 2109 Congress Avenue
Strong, A. J. ... 803½ San Felipe Street, Preston 4452
Walker, C. W. ... 3005 Dowling Street, Hadley 2558
Watson, Starkey ... 1018 Congress Avenue, Preston 1901
West, Taylor ... 214 San Jacinto Street
Williams, W. ... 2115 Nassau Street

Wilson, Lane   407½ Milam Street
Wilson, Sam   Basement Union National Bank Building, Preston 2756
Windell, P J   211 Milam Street
Woodson, James   68 Schrimpt Street
Wyatt, P B   Corner Congress and Austin Streets

BLACKSMITHS

Hubert, Jno W   701 N San Jacinto Street, Preston 2478
Hart, R A   1320 San Felipe, Hadley 4292
Hendrix, Charles   909 Crosby Street
Herald, A C   1019 San Felipe Street
Kemp, Frank   711 Smith Street, Preston 2772
Lee, Edward   2220 Clark Street
Oler & Gillmore   1007 Vine Street
McCullough, B S   1013 Dowling Street
Ward, C W   2502 Dallas Avenue, Preston 7707

BOARDING HOUSES

Brown, Rebecca   1206 Rice Street
Peters, Rosa   1603 Jackson Street, Hadley 4244

BOTTLING WORKS

Jones, Lacy   914 St Charles Street

BUSINESS COLLEGES

Branch, J C E   714½ Prairie Avenue

CAFES.

Dreamland Cafe (Young Bros, Proprietors)   613 San Felipe Street
Price's Cafe   620 San Felipe Street, Preston 2328

CABINET MAKERS

Williams, J E   1906 Live Oak Street

CEMENT BLOCK MANUFACTURERS

McGowan, Hattie, Mrs   1810 Velasco Street

CHARCOAL DEALERS

Johnson, D   2410 Anita Avenue

CHIMNEY SWEEPS

Bolton, Edward   3112 Clay Avenue
Koonts, E J   2801 Hutchins Street

CLOTHES CLEANERS AND PRESSERS

Adams, Jesse   716 Rusk Avenue
Allen, Della   1017 Dowling Street
Armstrong, Otis   1104 Schwartz Street
Austin, Roger   309 W 6th Street, Houston Heights
Battle & Adams   703 Prairie Avenue
Buckner, Clifton   3515 Dowling Street
Clark, C A   2714 Odin Avenue

Douglass & Billups   3018 Dowling Street
Echols, Caleb   1515 Prairie Avenue
Floyd, Benjamin   2317 Dallas Avenue, Preston 9873
Gorden & Thomas   2314 Congress Avenue
Griffin, Arlege   2805 Washington Avenue
Hayward, James A   2303 McKinney Avenue Preston 1930
Harrison, Haley   1913 Congress Avenue
Hardeway & Jorden   -   409 Milam Street
Harris, Hamilton   817 San Felipe Street
Henry John   2803 Odin Avenue
Hogg King   505½ San Felipe Street
Holland, Burl   2017 Congress Avenue
Houston, Henry   Basement Rossonian Apartments
Johnson, C J   712 Brazos Street, Preston 9702
Johnson, L C   511 La Branch Street
Jones, George   1417 Matthews Street
Logan, Joe   507 San Felipe Street, Preston 2413
Littlejohn, C L   421 San Felipe Street
Mitchell, Benjamin   1919 Hutchins Street
Morris, Henry   312½ San Felipe Street
Moss, Frank   803½ San Felipe Street
Nelson, James   902 Valentine Street
Overton, T V   1104 Schwartz Street, Preston 7938
Palm Beach Pressing Club   1217 Preston Avenue, Preston 3777
Richardson, H R   8 Allen Place
Simmons, Neal   618 San Felipe Street
Smith, Benjamin   1405 Milam Street
Smith, Tony   314 San Felipe Street Preston 7626
Spivey, Antonio   1807 Jackson Street
Stewart, O D   2312 Congress Avenue
Story, J L   918 Valentine Street, Preston 3258
Thomas, Harrison   2314 Congress Avenue
Thomas, Jefferson   11 Settegast Alley
Young, W F   609 Rusk Avenue

CONFECTIONERY AND FRUITS

Ellis, S E   915 San Felipe Street, Preston 5017
Foley, Wm   1012 San Felipe Street
Love, Felix   2717 Odin Avenue
Rogers, Charles   30th Avenue and Columbia Street, Independence Heights
Sadler & Sals   2515 Odin Avenue
White, Edward   1106½ Schwartz Street

CONTRACTORS AND BUILDERS

Bartley, W E   413½ Milam Street, Preston 3558
Bingham, Daniel & Son   1708 Cushing Street, Hadley 988
Bullock, James   2902 McGowen Avenue
Buttler, R H   2502 Anita Avenue Hadley 2458
Davis, B F   2018 Scott Street, Hadley 4175
Gunn, R G   2919 Drew Avenue, Hadley 4053
Hall, F H   1108 Palmer Street, Hadley 2723
Hodges, J L   501 Allston Street, Houston Heights
Jackson, J H   -   1704 Calhoun Avenue
Lewis, S D   2518 McGowen Avenue, Hadley 4031
White, K J   -   109 Denver Avenue
Young, Clarence   2701 Dowling Street, Hadley 302

DELICATESSEN

Price's Delicatessen   620 San Felipe Street, Preston 2328

DENTISTS

George, C A — 418½ Travis Street, Preston 5128
Cockrell, J L — 409½ Milam Street, Preston 1459

DRESSMAKERS

Bennett, Roberta — 815 St Charles Street
House, Earl — 404 Sabine Street
Keener, Estelle — 3419 Dowling Street
King, Julia A — 804 San Felipe Street, Preston 6626
Richer, Annie — 1910 Austin Street
Triplette, Belle — 1713 Edwards Street, Preston 7498

DRUGGISTS

Bayou City Drug Co — 411 Milam Street, Preston 121 and 2245
Climax Drug Co — 2018 Dowling Street, Hadley 610
Watts, P W — 815 Prairie Avenue, Preston 1397
Watts, P W — 2402 Dowling Street, Hadley 301

DRY GOODS AND NOTIONS

Harmon, J H — 423 San Felipe Street

EXPRESS AND DRAYAGE

Allen, Henderson — 3300 Velasco Street
Allen, Isiah — Scott and Anderson Streets
Bass, Grant — 2801 Polk Avenue
Baggley, John — 1110 St Charles Street
Bates, James — 314 San Felipe Street, Preston 7626
Bolden, Wm — Holt and Scott Streets
Cornelius, Edward — 2206 Edwards Street
Capitol Express Line — Corner Caroline and Texas, Preston 1792
Crawford, Jos — 2005 Spring Street
Cook, Jas — 3501 Broadway, Hadley 3222, Preston 870
DeBose, Wm — McGregor, 2 Blocks West of Velasco Street
Foster, Fields — 2723 Railroad Avenue
Foster, R G — 2509 Jefferson Avenue, Hadley 2991
Gomez, J F — 909 Maggie Street
Guy, Geo — 822 Oxford Street, Houston Heights
Hicks, John — 1121 Court Street
Holt, Gus — 3320 Broadway, Hadley 2502
Hunter, John — 3015 Dennis Avenue
Johnson, Armstrong — 1318 Granger Street
Johnson, D — 2410 Anita Avenue, Preston 870
Johnson, Edward — 2709 Live Oak Street
Johnson, Freeman — McGregor and Velasco Streets
Johnson, Warren — 2706 Live Oak Street
Jones, Lewis — 3104 McGowen Avenue
Kennedy, Lee — 2412 Polk Avenue
King, Israel — Elgin and Velasco Streets
Little, C H — 713 Railroad Avenue
Love, A J — 2203 Stevens Street, Preston 9405
Lynn, Henderson — Turner Avenue
Martin, Henry — 3119 Tuam Avenue
Mason, Sammie — 2304 State Street, Preston 6981
Miller, O M — 2902 Drew Avenue, Hadley 2419
Moore, J W — 622 Rutland, Houston Heights
Mumford, Wm — Wilson Addition
Penn, J B — 4610 Maxie Street
Perry, E M — 617 Larkin Street
Price, R J — 1109 Palmer Street
Roberts, Geo — 3002 McGowen Avenue

Seymour, R. T. .... 3012 Dennis Avenue
Simon, Henry .... 3217 Nance Street, Preston 7325
Smith, J. .... 1106 Decker Street, Hadley 2491
Speller, Geo. .... 3410 George Street
Strain, Wm. .... Wilson Addition
Surrell, John .... 1101 Summer Street, Preston 5109
Vinson, Henry .... 2903 Tuam Avenue, Hadley 3631
Williams, Charles .... Harrisburg Road
Williams, W. A. .... 1601½ Congress Avenue

FISH AND OYSTERS.

Galveston Fish & Oyster Co.   1014 San Felipe Street, Preston 2004

FURNISHED ROOMS.

Carter, J. H. .... 1109 Schwartz Street, Preston 7938
Freeman, Flora .... 1709 Tuam Avenue
Lively, Charlotte .... 903 Live Oak Street
Lyons, Clara .... 1402 Hutchins Street
Pero, Maria .... 2314 German Street
Red, Rachel .... 1717 St. Charles Street
Rhoads, Louis .... 906 Schwartz Street
Scott, H. T. .... 608 Prairie Avenue, Preston 7011
Speed, Holley .... 415 Smith Street
Waterhouse, Louise .... 1009 Rice Street

FURNITURE DEALERS AND REPAIRERS.

Fisher, E. W. D. .... 1119 Andrews Street
Fleming, Sandy .... 1913 Broadway
Miller, Sam .... 1007 San Felipe Street

GROCERS.

Allen, Wm. .... 1901 Live Oak Street, Hadley 2870
Anderson, J. H. .... 3111 Polk Avenue
Azie, F. S. .... 1816 Worm Street
Barlow, M. M. .... 3001 McGowen Avenue, Hadley 2235
Beverly, S. B. .... 2420 McKinney Avenue, Preston 6657
Bracey, Julia .... 2402 Scott Street
Brock, H. F. .... 2920 McGowen Avenue
Burton, Harris .... 3020 McGowen Avenue, Hadley 2723
Calhoun, D. C. .... 624 Allston Street, Houston Heights, Taylor 1484
Catchings, R. M. .... 2620 Rice Street, Hadley 3441
Clemmons, Joseph .... 801 W. 20th Avenue, Houston Heights
Cloud, Robert .... 1112 Shearn Street, Preston 4562
Cummings, Wm. .... 34th and Columbia Street
Delaney, Noah .... 3439 McGowen Avenue
Eldridge, T. L. .... 2819 Nance Street
Gilmore, J. S. .... 2619 Odin Avenue
Goodwin, D. .... 8th and Harris Streets, Wilson Addition
Green, S. R. .... 2609 Dowling Street

Hackley, Rene ....3501 Broadway
Harris, J. D. ....2719 Lamar Avenue
Hines, John ....1607 Robin Street
Horn & Son ....2121 Nassau Street, Taylor 103
Hudson, S. T. ....3002 Tuam Avenue
Jones, J. P. & Bros. ....2819 Dowling Street, Hadley 1825
Jones, L. J. ....2802 Scott Street, Hadley 1642
Jones, Sal. ....1619 Saulnier, Hadley 3862
Lane & Grays ....3309 Dowling Street, Hadley 1390
McGowan, Henry ....1419 Velasco Street
Maxwell, Wm. ....3401 McGowen Avenue, Hadley 2654
Miles, Annie ....902 W. 8th Avenue, Houston Heights
Miller, O. M. ....2902 Drew Avenue, Hadley 2419
Moose, Florence ....628 Railroad Street
Nesby, J. E. ....Fulton and Wall Streets, Hadley 4115
Parks, James ....Independence Heights
Reed, Albert ....613 San Felipe Street
Shepherd, A. L. ....2402 Dowling Street, Hadley 301
Sidner, S. J. ....1908 Hailey Street
Smith, Frank ....3105 Center, Taylor 2287
Stoney, James ....2918 Holman Avenue
Thomas, Lin ....912 Schwartz Street
Williams, D. ....Dennis and Sampson Streets, Hadley 1954
Wyndon, Wm. ....1715 Detroit Street

HACK AND CARRIAGE LINES.

Goodson, Geo. ....714½ Prairie Avenue, Preston 7929
Marshall, Cash ....1917 Hickory Street, Preston 7779
Marshall, Geo. ....Archer and Mellwood Streets, Taylor 1798
White, T. W. ....1511 Andrews Street, Preston 2713

HAIR DRESSERS.

Blunt, M. F. ....611 Robin Street
Brent, T. W., Miss ....1101 Dart Street, Preston 5009
Brown, Mary ....211 Robin Street, Preston 46
Grimes, J. V. ....2419 Chenevert Street
Watkins, Emma ....1607 Jackson St cc.

HAND LAUNDRY.
Collens, Geo. F. ....914 San Felipe Street, Preston 6455

HAT CLEANING AND BLOCKING.
Standard Tailoring, Cleaning & Pressing Co.   220 San Felipe Street, Preston 5667
Hayward, James A. ....2303 McKinney Avenue, Preston 1930

HOSPITAL.
Feagan, A. L. ....3102 Providence Street, Preston 2266

HOUSE MOVERS.
Cato, Wm. ....719 Heiner Street

ICE CREAM PARLOR.
Dreamland Parlor ....613 San Felipe Street

INSURANCE COMPANIES.

American Mutual Benefit Association

of HOUSTON, TEXAS

Phone Preston 3288.

Is a fraternal beneficiary association organized in the City of Houston. Was incorporated July 7. 1908. From its organization to December 31, 1914, it paid $62,352.50 for death benefits; $85,642.10 for sick benefits; total, $147.994.60. This organization bids fair to be one of the greatest institutions of its kind in America for and by colored people.

Founders and present officers are W. B. Cogle, President; F. T. Perkins, Vice-President; J. B. Grigsby, Treasurer, and Wm. Nickerson, Jr., Secretary.

Ancient Order of Pilgrims	413½ Travis Street, Preston 1338
First Texas State Insurance Co.	714½ Prairie Avenue, Preston 5446
Standard American Mutual Fire Insurance Co.	413½ Travis Street, Preston 2050

JEWELERS AND WATCHMAKERS.

Phillips, Joseph	1202½ San Felipe Street

MANICURES.

Manning, Sarah	Basement Union National Bank Bldg.
Taylor, Pearl	1017 Prairie Avenue

MEAT MARKETS.

Addison, J. C.	Independence Heights
Cummings, Wm.	Independence Heights
Hurd, Fred	2616 Hadley Avenue
Lane & Grays	3309 Dowling Street, Hadley 1390
McClellan, Geo.	2604 Live Oak Street
Scull, Richards	32d Street and Houston Avenue

MIDWIVES.

Hagen, Annie	609 Hobson Street, Preston 6728

MOTION PICTURES.

New Sun Set Theatre	711 San Felipe Street

NOTARIES.

Bartley, W. E.	413½ Travis Street, Preston 3558
Broyles, M. H.	714½ Prairie Avenue
Burgess, G. O.	Independence Heights
DeWalt, Olen P.	714½ Prairie Avenue, Preston 2599
Dickens, W. M. C.	409½ Milam Street, Preston 1459
Hardeway, J. J.	409½ Milam Street, Preston 2662
Perkins, F. T.	419½ Milam Street, Preston

NURSES

Burr, Louvenia	2402 Dallas Avenue, Preston 8263
Butler, L E	2502 Holman Avenue, Hadley 536
Foster Dona	Fulton Avenue and I & G N
Hagen, Annie	609 Hobson Street, Preston 6728
Johnson, Bessie	609 Hobson Street, Preston 6728

PHOTOGRAPHERS

Harris, C G	811 San Felipe Street, Preston 5960

PHYSICIANS AND SURGEONS

Covington, B J	409½ Milam Street, Preston 6436
Davis Dr	411 Milam Street, Bayou City Drug Store
Durham, E A	411½ Travis Street, Preston 4691
Ferrell, R F	409½ Milam Street, Preston 1184
Garrett, O C	417 Robin Street, Preston 8149
Lee, H E	413½ Travis Street
Lindsay, J H T	409½ Travis Street
Ramsey, E B	419½ Milam Street

PRODUCE

Keener, O E	3419 Dowling Street

PRINTERS

McKinney, Van H	411½ Travis Street, Preston 5039

PUBLISHERS

Pendleton, James	419½ Milam Street, Preston 5493
Western Star Publishing Co	419½ Milam Street, Preston 4338

REAL ESTATE

Broyles, M H	714½ Prairie Avenue
DeWalt, O P	714½ Prairie Avenue, Preston 2599
Edwards Land Co	418½ Travis Street, Preston 5120
Green, C H	2701 Mills Street
Hardeway J J	409½ Milam Street, Preston 2662
Lee, Rob	411½ Travis Street

RESTAURANTS

Anderson, James	1013 San Felipe Street
Anderson, Lucy	720 Waverly Street
Anderson, Wm	94 Gable Street
Bates, Frank	304 Dowling Street
Bayou City Cafe	411 Milam Street
Booker, Viola	90 Gable Street
Born, Jackson	403 Sabine Street
Boykin, Eli	2105 German Street
Briaggs, Willie	2619 Leona Street
Brown, Clara	31st Street and Houston Avenue
Brown, John	1904 Runnels Street
Brown, Taylor	2806 Washington Avenue
Carter, Jessie B	2501 McKinney Avenue
Carter, Mattie	3418 Dowling Street
Clark, Jessie	3100 Center Street
Clark, R C	2504 McKinney Avenue
Council Cora	5519 Washington Avenue
Crahan, Flida	813 San Felipe Street
Dickson & McDuffy	2713½ Odin Avenue

Dixon, Wm	1409 Clark Street
Doin, J H	1307 Congress Avenue
Eagleton, Peter	312 San Felipe Street
Ellis, Louis	1019 North San Jacinto Street
Figgins, Martha	1220 Paige Street
Foster, Porter	2207 Commerce Avenue
Gordon, S D	1101 Frederick Street.
Guiton, Sarah	85 Marsh Street
Haves, Sherman	1411 Andrews Street
Henderson, J E	2017 Dowling Street
Hunter, Elizabeth	3204 Washington Avenue
Jackson, Francis	716 San Felipe Street
James Charlotte	1909½ Whitty Street
Johnson, T J	924 Andrews Street
Jordan, Wm	3115 Dallas Avenue
Keys, Wm	2201 Holman Avenue
Lewis, Ella	Independence Heights
Lewis, Ernest	911 Hobson Street
McDonald, Adeline	742 West 22nd Street
McGee, Delphia	316 Walker Avenue
McGowan, Elizabeth	2812 Dallas Avenue
Mason, Annie	2604½ Washington Avenue
Matthews, Eliza	1418 Matthews Street
Matthews, Geo	2620 Dallas Avenue
Micheau & O'Brien	2416 Pierce Avenue
Mitchell, Frank	807 West 8th Avenue
Mock, Leonard	704 Paige Street
Pardell, Cora	2515 Prairie Avenue
Perry, Lula	3010 Cline Street
Parnell, Pinkie	1205 Palmer Street
Price, Andrew	3030 Washington Avenue
Reed, Isom	1901½ Runnels Street
Robinson, Horace	708 Andrews Street
Ross, Georgie	1001 Andrews Street
Scott, Abraham	2406 McKinney Avenue
Sharp, L B	1011 Brown Street
Sims, J M	2729 Glass Street
Smith, Lee	1202 Liberty Avenue
Smith, Wm	2818 Nance Street
Smith & Elka	710 Preston Avenue
Sterling, Adolphus	1102 Schwartz Street
Taylor, R C	1019 Vine Street
Vincent, W F	2803½ Odin Avenue
Vinson, Mattie	2603 Engelke Street
Washington, Hattie	5506 Washington Avenue
Watson, Israel	1617 Dowling Street
White, C F	803 House Street
White, Effie	801 West 6th Avenue
Whittaker, John	1611 San Felipe Street
Williams, Dolly	2712½ Odin Avenue
Williams & Roberts	3001 Dowling Street
Williams, Douglass	3103 Tennessee Street
Williams Lillie	2806 Odin Avenue
Woodson, Jas	68 Schrimpf Street
Wright, Clayton	3119 Barron Street

SHOEMAKERS

Branch, Horace	1904 Runnels Street
Crooms, L H	816 San Felipe Street
Thomas, Samuel	1606 Wilson Street

SHOE SHINING STANDS

Harris, Hamilton	817 San Felipe Street
Jones, Van	603½ San Felipe Street
Perry, Henry	2716 Odin Avenue
Thomas, Fletcher	817 Congress Avenue

We never close Try us when others fail you.

Ward, J A	1419 Congress Avenue

SHOOTING GALLERIES

Scott & Lomax	413 Milam Street
Versa, Joseph	1902 Runnels Street

TAILORS

Band, R C	419½ Milam Street
Clark, C A	2714½ Odin Avenue
Davis, Geo	907 Leeland Avenue
King, J W	1006 McKinney Avenue
Hayward, J A	2303 McKinney Avenue, Preston 1930
Houston Custom Tailors	2414 McKinney Avenue, Preston 9420
Parris, L J	2002 Dowling Street
Ross, A S	418½ Travis Street, Preston 5120
Simmons, C C	509 San Felipe Street
Standard Tailoring, Cleaning & Pressing Co	220 San Felipe Street Preston 5667
Turner, A R	1215 Preston Avenue

UNDERTAKERS

Frierson & Co	201-3 San Felipe Street
Jackson, E	1017 San Felipe Street
Williams, A	3014 Liberty Avenue

WOOD DEALERS

Harris, R B	2006 Dowling Street
Hartley, E H	1506 Wickman Street
Lawson, Thomas	3017 Houston Avenue
Lee, E	411½ Travis Street
Perry, E H	3010 Cline Street
Sessums, A C	1120 San Felipe Street
Sledge, Willis	2710 Opelousas Street
Smith, Charles	317 Ruthven Street
Spriggs, Ellis	513 Rutland Street
Watson, Green	711 Railroad Street
Whitehead, Tobias	3201 Roanoke Street
Whitehead, Walter	2719 Opelousas Street

PRAIRIE VIEW NORMAL AND INDUSTRIAL COLLEGE

PRAIRIE VIEW, TEXAS

PRAIRIE VIEW NORMAL AND INDUSTRIAL COLLEGE
By NAT Q. HENDERSON

The Prairie View State Normal and Industrial College was organized under an act to provide for the organization and support of a normal school at Prairie View, Waller County, for the preparation and training of colored teachers, which act was approved April 19, 1879, and provided the Prairie View State Normal and Industrial College shall be under the control and supervision of the Board of Directors of the Agricultural and Mechanical College of Texas.

Aside from the preparation and training of teachers for the colored schools of Texas, Prairie View aims to impart something of the scholarly spirit indispensable to excellence in teaching, and to awaken an enthusiasm for the education and for the industrial and moral improvement of the colored race in Texas.

Believing in the value of industrial training in connection with the literary and professional studies as a means to mental, moral and economic improvement, the Board of Directors are from time to time adding to the agricultural and mechanical departments, a department of female industries is provided.

COURSES OF STUDY.

The instruction of students is committed to a faculty which is organized into departments, as follows: Mathematics, English, Science, Pedagogy and History, Mechanics, Agriculture, Dress Making and Millinery and Cooking.

Special mention is made of the Department of Agriculture. The aim of this course is to prepare better farmers, farm managers, demonstrators and teachers. The College has 1,700 acres of land at the disposal of this department to show the students every phase of farm life—hay making, syrup making, watermelon growing; in fact, one of the chief aims of the department is to grow every kind of plant possible so as to acquaint the student with the best methods of culture.

The common diseases of animals and the care of the same is given strict attention.

MECHANICAL DEPARTMENT.

The great object of this department is to foster a high appreciation of the value and dignity of labor. The students are trained in the use of the various tools employed in the mechanic arts, and are thus given a good foundation in manual training, which will enable them to teach the arts in the schools in which they may be employed.

SHORT COURSES.

In order to afford an opportunity for the young people to prepare themselves for usefulness in the industrial development of the State, several short courses in the trades have been introduced. These courses have been introduced more for those of mature age and for those whose responsibility will not allow them to spend a greater length of time in the institution. Most of these courses are of one year's duration. Students who complete the studies of the full course satisfactorily will receive a Normal Diploma, which has by law the rank of a permanent teachers' certificate, and is valid during good behavior.

First Grade Normal Certificates, valid for six years, and Second Grade, valid for three years, are issued to those who complete the required subjects and attain the required standing in the work of the third and second years.

RELIGIOUS OBSERVANCES.

On Sunday morning Sunday School is regularly held. Two voluntary Christian societies are maintained by the students, the Y. W. C. A. for girls and the Young Men's Christian Association for young men. Two meetings are held by each association every week to study the Bible as outlined by the International Committee, and to discuss different religious and moral subjects. At 7 p. m. every Sunday students assemble in the chapel to hear a religious lecture or sermon.

DISCIPLINE.

The discipline of the school aims to lead students to self-control and to prepare them for the successful discharge of the practical duties of school, from shop to home.

The careers of the students from this institution show that these ends are being attained.

The enrollment each year is around the 1,000 mark, and as soon as increased facilities are afforded the enrollment will increase.

Texas Negroes and the State have just occasion to feel proud of the work of this great school

Foster Hall   Kirby Hall   Agricultural Building

Mess Hall and Chapel   Administration Building

Girls' Dormitories

Luckie Hall

Key To Group On Opposite Page

1—E. L. Blackshear
2—C. H. Waller, B. S.
3—William Cook
3½—Miss Martha C. Moxley
4—Miss Kate Fulton
5—Miss Ruth Cox
6—E. W. Scott
7—Mrs. S. E. Hancock
8—Armstrong Lewis
9—Napoleon B. Edward
10—P. E. Bledsoe, B. S.
11—Mrs. Ethel L. McGee
12—A. Richardson
13—T. H. Brittain
14—Miss M. J. Sims
15—Charles Atherton
16—Miss A. L. Evans
17—Miss C. B. Drisdale
18—Miss W. B. Patterson

19—J. R. Adams
20—Miss Ophelia Robinson
21—G. O. Sanders
22—N. A. Banks, Ph. D.
23—R. L. Isaacs
24—G. W. Buchanan
25—Mrs. Sophronia McCall
26—H. J. Mason
27—A. Day, Jr.
28—A. D. Ewell
29—Mrs. N. R. Crawford
30—C. H. Griggs, A. B.
31—W. A. Blackshear
32—J. T. Hodges, A. B.
33—W. P. Terrell, B. S.
34—J. E. Stamps, A. B.
35—H. Aldridge
36—James W. Bartlett

EDWARD L BLACKSHEAR

Edward L Blackshear, born at Montgomery, Alabama. September 8, 1862, finished the Swayne High School course at the age of 12 years Prof J F McPherion, one of his teachers, a Northern man, became interested in young Blackshear and induced him to attend Tabor College in Iowa where young Blackshear lived with Prof A S McPherion, brother of Prof J F McPherion He completed the college course in six years and came to Texas in 1882 He spent two years teaching in the county schools of Ellis and Bastrop counties and working with a telephone gang, setting poles between Waco and Gatesville In 1883 he was elected principal of the ward schools for colored people in the City of Austin He taught in Austin for thirteen years, occupying successfully the positions of principal in a primary school principal of grammar school and supervisor of city schools

In 1896 he was elected as principal of the Prairie View State Normal and Industrial College He is one of the most forceful and strongest educators in the Negro race He is a member of the National Association of Teachers in colored schools and a Fellow of the American Association for the advancement of Science, President of the Texas State Negro Farmers' Congress, as well as of the National Negro Farmers' Congress, which national congress was organized in Birmingham, Ala , July 4, 1913, and holds its second biennial meeting at San Francisco, August 26 to 29, 1915

PERSONNEL OF PRAIRIE VIEW STATE NORMAL AND INDUSTRIAL COLLEGE

Adams, J R —1872, Carpenter, Prairie View Born in Tennessee Graduate of University of Nashville in 1900 Married to Miss Katie Guilham in 1906 Member of Masons, two years assistant superintendent of construction

Aldridge, H C —Steward, Prairie View Born in Kentucky , owns city property Married Miss Ida Cooper in 1903 Member of the M E Church, Past Master Mason, U B T , S M T Steward for 20 years

Banks, N A —1860; Teacher, Prairie View Born in East Liberty, Ohio Graduate of B S & M S of Wilberforce and Ph D of Paul Quinn Married Miss Emma A Woods in 1890 Has one child Member A M E Church, P M of Masons, U B F , P C of K of P , P C M of K of T , President State Teachers' Association Taught 30 years in public schools Chaplain of Prairie View Normal and Secretary of faculty Head Department of Mathematics Taught in Prairie View eight years Professor of Higher Mathematics in Paul Quinn College for eight years Principal of Palestine High School for nine years Collaborator with son in textbook on Geometry now in preparation for press

Bartlett, Jas W —Teacher Prairie View Normal Born in Falls County, Texas, in 1875 Graduate in the Literary Course Hearne Academy and Normal Course Prairie View Normal Associate Professor Mathematics Prairie View past two years , formerly vice-principal Waco High School Conducted five successful summer normals Formerly engaged in newspaper work at Marlin Married Miss Ola V Estelle in 1900 Owns home in Waco Member Baptist Church and P C Masons

Blackshear, W A —1891, Teacher, Prairie View Born in Austin Texas Graduate of Prairie View in 1907 Member of Masons Taught in public schools three years at present assistant in Department of Mechanics

Bledsoe Paul E —1867, Teacher Prairie View Born at Fayetteville Ala Graduate of Talledega College and Central University of Indiana in 1887 Property consists of nice home Married to Miss Annie Dell Harrison in 1890 Member of Congregational Church Member of G U O O F and Mason

Brittain T H —1885, Teacher, Prairie View Born in Nations, Texas Graduate of Tuskegee in 1905 Property consists of real estate Married to Miss Katie Blanch Montgomery in 1911 Member of Missionary Baptist Church Member of Masons and U B F Head of Manual Training Department for nine years

Buchanan, G W —Teacher, address Prairie View, Texas   Born in Marshall, Texas   Graduate of Prairie View, class 1912   Owns farm and city property   Married to Miss Ruth Lester in 1901   Member of the Missionary Baptist Church, Odd Fellows and U B F   Taught in the public schools and three years a Prairie View State Normal Professor of History

Cook, Wm —Foreman Printing Department   Native of Texas   Born 1878   Married 1890   Four years at Prairie View and 30 years a printer

Cox, Miss Ruth E —Born in Mexia, Texas   Graduate of the Literary and Industrial Department, Sewing and Millinery Department, Prairie View Normal 1909   Teacher in the Domestic Art Department, Prairie View   Taught one year in the public schools of Freestone County, Texas   Member of the A M E Church

Crawford Mrs N R —Teacher in Prairie View Normal   Born in Houston in 1865   Graduate Prairie View in 1908   Owns city and farm property   Member of the Trinity M E Church, Houston   Member Eastern Star and A O O P   Teacher of Science Prairie View, and teacher 10 years in Houston public schools

Day, Aaron, Jr —1891, Teacher Prairie View Normal and Industrial Institute   Born at Dayton, Texas   Graduate of Prairie View in 1910   Member A M E Church   Three years assistant professor of Chemistry in Prairie View Normal and Industrial Institute

Drisdale, Miss C B —1885, Teacher, Prairie View   Born in Blum, Texas   Graduate of Prairie View in 1905   Property consists of nice home   Member of Missionary Baptist Church   Formerly taught in Austin public schools

Edward, Napoleon B —Teacher and Poet   Born in Gonzales, Texas   Graduate of the Gonzales High School and Prairie View Normal   Specialized in Languages   Successful teacher in the public schools of the State for over 10 years   Connected with Prairie View for past four years   At present assistant professor of Latin and English   Member of Providence Baptist Church, Gonzales, K P and U B F   Author of two books of poems, "Lyrics" and "Lyrics of Life and Love"

Evans, Miss Annie L —Teacher and Dean of Women's Department, Prairie View   Associate Professor and Head Preceptress   Member of the Methodist Church, U B F and King's Daughters   Student of Oberlin College and University of Chicago

Ewell A D —1865, Instructor Steam Laundry and Hat Manufacturing, of Prairie View   Born at McKinney, Texas   Educated in common schools   Owns home and farm property   Married to Rosie Lee Warner in 1902   Member Masons, 32nd degree Scottish Rite, Order of Mystic Shrine   Studied in New York and Connecticut

Fulton, Miss Katie V —Teacher   Born Fayetteville Tenn   Graduate of Domestic Arts, Prairie View   Past three years teacher of Domestic Art, Prairie View   Three years Supervisoress of the Jean Fund in Lee County, Texas, with the best record of any teacher   Took summer course in Industrial Arts   Member A M E Church   Home, Belton, Texas

Griggs, C H —Teacher   Born at Baton Rouge, La , in 1863   Graduate Bishop College in 1885, A B and Guadaloupe College   Owns city property   Married Miss Fannie Abner in 1886   Member of the Missionary Baptist Church, Assistant Grand Secretary U B F , Knights of Pythias, P C and P D , United Order of Odd Fellows and Mason   Head Department of History and Pedagogy and Dean of Men for past six years   Principal of the Conroe College and principal of the Cuero High School for 20 years

Hancock, Mrs S E —Teacher, Prairie View   Born at Austin, Texas   Student of Oberlin College   City property in Austin   Member of Congregational Church, A M W and F I H   Head matron three years Domestic Science

Hodges, Jas P—Teacher   Born Gonzales in 1869 Graduate Prairie View 1889 Graduate Atlanta University in 1894 with A B Degree   Owns 371 acres farm land   Married to Emma Morton in 1896   Member Missionary Baptist Church   Now head of the Department of English and Latin, manager Students' Exchange, Librarian Prairie View

Howard, C Gertrude—Born in St Paul, Minn   Took course in the University of Minnesota and the College of Agriculture   Taught one year at Tuskegee Institute and for the past two years in the Domestic Science Department, Prairie View Normal and Industrial College

Isaac, R L—Teacher   Born at Oakland Texas, in 1872   Graduate of Prairie View in 1893   Owns 300 acres farm land   Married Miss M E Sims in 1901   Member of the M E Church, Past Master Masons, Treasurer Prairie View State Normal past two years   Associate Professor of Mathematics eight years   Assistant five years   Member Board of Directors Student Life Insurance Company of Atlanta, Ga , Board of Directors Electrical Indicators, Director College Business and Trust Co

Johnson, R F—1889, Shoemaking, Prairie View   Born at Minerva, Texas   St Louis factory training   Property consists of home   Member of Antioch Baptist Church Mason   Instructor in shoemaking for eight years

Lewis, Armstrong—1889, Blacksmithing, Prairie View   Born in Georgia   Graduate of Tuskegee in 1911   City property   Member of Wesley Chapel, Houston, Grand United Order of Odd Fellows and P C F   Instructor in Blacksmithing and Wheelwright

Mason, H J—Born in 1886 at Hockley Texas Graduate in college course in Wiley College   Member of the M E Church and Farmers' Improvement Society   Taught one year in English Department, Prairie View Normal   At present is secretary to the President   Formerly assistant business manager Southwestern Christian Advocate

McCall, Mrs Saphronia—Head Nurse, Prairie View Hospital past three years   Born 1877   Native Texan   Graduate of the Provident Hospital, Chicago, Ill , 1911.   Owns home   Member of the M E Church

McGee, Mrs Ethel—Widow   Born at Wilberforce, Ohio   Educated in the Wilberforce University   Graduate in Domestic Art and Domestic Science   For past two years teacher in Domestic Science Department, Prairie View Normal   Member of the A M E Church

Moxley, Miss Martha C—Teacher, Prairie View   Born at Corsicana, Texas   Graduate of Prairie View in 1914   Member Missionary Baptist Church   For past year assistant music teacher

Patterson Miss W B—Teacher, Prairie View   Born at Calvert, Texas   Graduate of Washington Normal and Washington College of Music in 1909   Member M E Church Music teacher and directress of Prairie View chorus

Richardson, A —Head of Tailoring Department Born at Evansville, Wis in 1880 Address, Prairie View, Texas   Graduate of Prairie View, Evansville High School and Tuskegee Institute in 1905   Owns house and lot   Married Miss Nancy Thompkins in 1914   Member Congregational Church   Member Masons   Connected with Prairie View three years   Formerly instructor in Tailoring at Topeka College

Robinson, Miss O A —Born in Jackson County, Texas   Educated in the public schools of Victoria, Texas, and graduate of Mary Allen Seminary   Taught in Mary Allen Seminary and rural schools for 12 years   Teacher in the English Department, Prairie View for the past three years   Member of the M E Church and Farmers' Improvement Society   Owns home

Sanders, Gaston O —1878 Mechanical and Electrical Engineer, Prairie View Normal and Industrial Institute Born at San Diego Cal Graduate of Tillotson College in 1899 Post-Graduate Streight University   Married to Pearl W Washington in 1904 Trustee M E Church, K R and S K of P, Secretary Masons Benevolent Association seven years Spanish and French interpreter United States Immigration Service Two years with Prairie View Family of six children

Scott, E W —1886, Teacher, Prairie View, Texas Born in Belton Texas Graduate of Prairie View Normal and Industrial Institute 1912 Owns 125 acres of farm land in Bell County Married to Miss Violet V Jackson in 1901 Past Secretary of Masons Member Odd Fellows Member M E Church Head of Broom and Mattress Department Three years in this position Formerly taught in State D D & B Institute at Austin, and taught for several years in public schools

Simms, Miss M J —Teacher, Prairie View Born in Austin Graduate of Prairie View in 1890. Property consists of nice home Member of Missionary Baptist Church Member of U B F, S M T, Young Women's Christian Association, Assistant Preceptress Young Women's Christian Association

Terrell, Prof W P —Address, Prairie View, Texas Born at Fort Worth, Texas, in 1884 Head Mechanical Department, Prairie View Graduate of Kansas State Agricultural College, 1904, and Massachusetts Institute of Technology Married Miss R E L Lyman in 1914 Junior Deacon Masons, member Missionary Baptist Church Associate member American Institute Electricity Nine years with Prairie View

Waller, C H —1905, Professor of Agriculture Born at Macon, Ga, in 1880 Graduate Pennsylvania State College, 1905, and South Carolina State College in 1898 Owns $3,000 00 worth of property Married Miss Annie M Walton in 1908 Member Presbyterian Church, Masons A Z, F I S Taught at Tuskegee Head of Science Department, Haines Institute, Augusta, Ga Head of the Agricultural Department of Prairie View four years

Wood, A T —1889, Agricultural Department, Prairie View Normal Prairie View Born at Rusk, Texas Graduate of Prairie View in 1912 Member of Missionary Baptist Church, Masons, K of P, I C Professor of Agronomy Taught in public school at Rusk, Texas

THE CAPABILITY OF THE NEGRO RACE
By Prof. E. L. Blackshear
Foremost Negro in Texas Cites Proof to Show Progress Being Made

During the war between the States, that war whose battle of Gettysburg marks the climax of all that was romantic and chivalric in war as poetically conceived in contrast to the purely mechanical and impersonal carnage of the present great war in Europe, the Morril act was passed by the Congress of the United States and signed by the immortal President Lincoln. This act was introduced by Senator Morril of Vermont and its passage attracted little notice at the time, engrossed as the nation was in the interest arising out of the States. Yet the Morril act was wholly unique in the history of civilization. Never before had such sums been spent for mechanical and agricultural education in the schools of a people. Each of the States became entitled to a free appropriation of $25,000 annually. A subsequent act of Congress has increased this sum to $50,000 annually for each State. Thus a vast work of popular practical education was inaugurated, and in all the Southern States it was made obligatory that a part of this money should be spent for the colored people of these States and on this foundation rests the establishment and maintenance of Southern State colleges for Negro youth including the Prairie View State Normal and Industrial College. Thus do we, the Negroes of the South, owe to the wisdom, foresight and broad-minded spirit of Senator Justin Morril of Vermont a debt of imperishable gratitude and profound respect as one of the great builders of American civilization.

MANY HELPS FOR EDUCATIONAL MOVEMENT.

But the Morril fund is not the only agency that is responsible for the inauguration of the educational movement among the Negro people of the South. We owe a debt to the organized Christianity of this nation we could never have repaid except as we have taken advantage of the opportunities which the American Christian denominations have offered us and still offer us in schools established as Christian educational missions among the Negro people. The Methodist Episcopal Church, South, Southern Presbyterians, the Northern Methodist, Baptist and Presbyterians, the Christian Church, Roman Catholic and Congregationalist have all contributed to the education and civilization as well as to the evangelization of the Negroes of the United States. Such institutions as Fisk, Walden at Nashville, Straight and Leland at New Orleans, Atlanta, Clark and Atlanta Baptist College at Atlanta, Emerson at Mobile, Chaflin at Orangeburg, S. C., Shaw at Raleigh, Talladega College in Alabama, the Hartshorn Memorial College and Virginia Union Seminary at Richmond, Bishop and Wiley at Marshall, Texas, Tillotson and Samuel Houston at Austin and Mary Allen at Crockett, Texas, have exerted an inestimable influence in Christianizing as well as educating the Negroes and in lightening that historic burden which the white man bears in all lands and zones of the globe. Nor should we fail to mention the many institutions established and sustained by Negroes themselves with little, of any, outside aid, of which the Central Texas College at Waco, the Industrial College at Fort Worth, and Houston College are excellent examples.

SIGNIFICANT HISTORY OF NEGRO EDUCATION.

But no less significant in the brief but interesting history of Negro education has been the rise and growth of what is known as industrial education as first inaugurated by General Armstrong in army barracks at Hampton, Virginia, and which has since become the Hampton Institute of national fame. This industrial idea of education born in the brain of a Christian Federal officer, General Armstrong, who was born the son of missionary parents in the Hawaiian Islands, was taken up by his great pupil, Booker T. Washington, a slave child of the hills of West Virginia, and popularized by successful exemplification at the Tuskegee institution and by skillful delineation on the lecture platform and in the public press and printed page that industrial education has become the theme of the hour not only for Negroes but for whites as well. It is Dr. Washington himself who tells in his inimitable way how when the white man takes over an occupation formerly monopolized by Negroes he always gives a new name to the occupation which at the same time he refines and improves. Thus the black man's barber shop becomes the white man's tonsorial parlors and Uncle Sambo's whitewashing become Mr. George's kalsomining and artistic mural decoration. And now Dr. Washington's simple industrial training has become for the white man, vocational education viewed in its varied psychological, economic, historic, physiological, ethical, esthetic and social phases. However, jesting aside, this is one secret of the white man's progress—his wonderful ability to analyze thought, a process or phenomenon and throw these parts into new and amazing synthesis. Dr. Washington's conception of industrial education for the Negro and of its relation to the South's economic possibilities and welfare met with instant approval from white people North and South but as for us, his own people, the plan of industrial education met with strong opposition for a number of years.

THE VICTORY OF BOOKER T. WASHINGTON

But today the victory of Dr. Washington's propaganda is well nigh complete, but the trouble so far as Negroes are concerned is that equipment for industrial education is expensive, and trained teachers of the industrial arts are few and far between. Among the white Americans North and South, there is no longer any doubt as to the value of industrial education and vast sums are spent annually to equip the white boy to meet the industrial needs of his day. While although all acknowledge now that industrial education is the great need of the Negro youth, yet but little is really being adequately undertaken in their behalf except in a few progressive cities like Houston, where under the influence of that prince among educators and Christian leaders, philosophers and statesmen, Hon. P. W. Horn, much has already been undertaken and still greater things may be hoped for. Yet in many places small beginnings are being made, inaugurated out of which the needful facilities may develop. One thing is certain he who opposes industrial education for the colored people is indeed blind and can not read the signs of the time. Of all races we need most to revise our estimate of the dignity and value of labor and to acquire a permanent conception of the true relation of labor to health, wealth and morals. If there is ever to be an aristocracy of our race let it be that of those who are industrious and at the same time morally decent—an aristocracy of honest thrift and not one of sham and pretense and mere aping of the extravagances of the white race. Indeed, we should emulate the less obvious and really fundamental qualities of the white race on which its progress has rested—the stern qualities of thrift, character, economy, will-power and self-mastery. Of all the peoples we need most, for example, the simple lessons of saving and economy, of present self-sacrifice for the future good.

WHAT DR. KNAPP ACCOMPLISHED

We turn aside from the consideration of the movement of industrial education with which the name of Dr. Washington will be forever closely associated to that of another related movement inaugurated in the South by a Northern man whose name will live always in the memories and affections of the white South, a man whose achievements, however, have had a far-reaching effect on both races and on all sections of our common country. I refer, of course, to Dr. Seaman Knapp, and I quote verbatim a brief sketch of his work taken from the recently issued report of the General Education Board 1902-1914, a valuable document which may be had free by addressing General Education Board, 61 Broadway, New York, N. Y. Says this report.

The Mexican boll weevil was just beginning its devastations. As the pest spread, a panic had taken place in Texas. Cotton was the principal crop, and the days of its profitable cultivation seemed to be numbered. Farms were abandoned and counties nigh depopulated. Acting for the United States Department of Agriculture, Dr. Knapp in 1903 established a community demonstration farm at Terrell, Texas, for the purpose of showing farmers how cotton could be raised despite the boll weevil, with such success, indeed, that from one point of view, the boll weevil curse proved a sort of blessing in disguise.

By means of the improved methods employed by Dr Knapp, the production of cotton was actually increased and normal business conditions were accordingly restored

Dr Knapp's procedure was the very essence of simplicity He knew that through seed selection and intensive farming the productivity of lands could be immensely augmented, in a word, more could be gained through intelligence than was lost through the weevil In every afflicted vicinity Dr Knapp undertook to propagate his methods by actual "demonstration" of their value

DR KNAPP'S PLAN SIMPLE ONE

Selecting a relatively capable farmer in a given neighborhood, Dr Knapp induced him to plant and cultivate a certain amount of land in a certain way with a certain kind of seed, he relied on the natural imitative instinct to induce others to follow when once the result called attention to the superiority of the process Its bearing in the field was characteristic and inimitable Approaching the farmer whom he desired to interest, he carried on a dialogue somewhat in this fashion

"I have a cotton seed," he would explain, "which has been carefully selected through a long series of years The planting of this seed and its proper cultivation will more than double your yield of cotton

"We have come to you as a leading farmer of this vicinity and would like to have you make demonstration of its value The demonstration, we believe, will not only convince you of the value of good seed and of scientific tillage, but will also teach your neighbors the same thing "

Interest once aroused and confidence gained, the necessary conditions were broached one by one The land must be plowed in the fall "Why?" Because fall plowing gives mellowness to the soil and affords nature an opportunity to prepare plant food for the coming season Moreover, the rows of cotton must be planted wide apart "Why?" Because 85 per cent or more of all vegetation is light and air, if the rows are close together the cotton is starved and smothered Again, the cotton must be cultivated six or eight times "Why?" Because there is plenty of moisture down by the roots and you can keep it there only by constantly breaking up the soil so that it may not be evaporated by the heat of the sun Thus the demonstration was in the first instance a simple object lesson A few shrewd aphorisms controlled Dr Knapp's procedure "Don't confuse the people by elaborate programs, the average man like the crow, can not count more than three" And again, "Do the next thing" He formulated and widely circulated

TEN AGRICULTURAL COMMANDMENTS

1   The removal of all surplus water on and in the soil
2   Deep fall plowing, and in the South a winter crop (oats, wheat, etc)
3   The best seed including variety and quality
4   Proper spacing of plants
5   Intensive cultivation and systematic rotation of crops
6   The judicious use of barnyard manure, legumes and commercial fertilizers
7   The home production of the food required for the family and for the stock
8   The use of more horsepower and better machinery
9   The raising of more and better stock, including the cultivation of grasses and forage plants
10   Keeping an accurate account of the cost of the farm operations

Such, in brief, is the General Education Board's sketch of the work of the immortal Seaman Knapp, and in this work is seen the germ of that great extension work which is the fruit of the congressional effort of a great South Carolina statesman, Hon Mr Lever and the methods of this work will be but the extension to every phase of rural life in the United States of the methods of the late lamented Dr Seaman Knapp

THE LEVER FUND EPOCHAL ADVANCE

Unlike the Morrill fund however, the Lever fund, which will place at the disposal of the States ultimately a total of several millions of dollars for extension work among the people on the farm, conditioned on each State's appropriation of a sum equal to what it receives from the Federal government, the Lever fund act did not make it obligatory that a share of what each State receives should be spent for the benefit of the Negro people In Alabama a part of the Lever fund has, however, been set apart for the Negroes, and in Texas Hon Clarence Ousley, director of extension, announces that a part of the Lever fund allotted Texas will probably be spent among the Negroes Yet even though no part of the Lever fund were spent in any State specifically for work among Negroes, still will the Negroes benefit by the example of their white neighbors and by information gained directly and indirectly from them Knowledge, like light, has a way of sending its ray in all directions, and, like life itself, has its own modes of propagation, when once it gets started on its way In this great nation, where the white light of science beats down in mighty floods of radiation upon all her institutions of art, of learning, of religion and of civilization, it will be strange indeed if the black people do not catch some ray of its benefits in every department of human thought and human endeavor, do not catch at least some crumbs falling from the groaning festal board of truth where the fruits of investigation increase in richness and abundance from hour to hour A practical proof of such generalization is seen in the report of the General Education Board, page 54, on "Farm Demonstration Work Among Negro Farmers," which reads

"DEMONSTRATION WORK AMONG NEGRO FARMERS

"The Negro farmer has been quick to take advantage of such opportunities in demonstration work as have been offered to him by the agents In his very first report Dr Knapp writes As the bulk of cotton crops is produced by colored laborers and tenants, all of our agents are not only instructed but of their own choice select colored farmers as demonstrators, visiting them regularly and giving them every attention ' In some States, colored local agents work under white State agents At Mound Bayou, in the delta region of Mississippi, under a colored local agent, six demonstrators were started in 1907, 41 were in operation the next year and the sum of $50 was raised for colored people themselves for prizes In Virginia a somewhat different plan is pursued, a district agent reporting directly to Washington being in charge Hampton and Tuskegee Institutes and many other industrial and agricultural schools for Negroes have played essential parts in this development Their training has produced agents and teachers, who go out into life persuaded that the fate of the race depends primarily on improved economic efficiency Frequently, throughout the year, the Negro farmers of the neighborhood or State are brought together to see and to value each other s product Pride and solidarity are thus built upon "

DEMONSTRATION AMONG NEGROES

The precise results due to demonstration efforts among Negro farmers are difficult to give, because many colored farmers are enrolled under white agents, but the number of colored agents is gradually increasing In 1910 there were 23 next year 32 At the latter date 3,709 Negro farmers were reported by name, and it was estimated by the department that 20,000 were under instruction The results were as good as those obtained by the whites In South Carolina, for example (where, by the way, 56 per cent of the farms are operated by Negroes without white supervision), there were, in 1911, 570 acres of cotton and 449 acres of corn under demonstration by Negroes

The average yield per acre throughout the State was 795 pounds of seed cotton and 18 2 bushels of corn ` The Negro demonstrators averaged 1567 9 pounds of seed cotton and 38 1 bushels of corn The gain in money at current price approximateed $24,000

Among Negroes as among whites the work tends to expand in scope Demonstrators are instructed to procure information regarding the rural economy of the Negro farmers how many plow in the fall, have summer and winter gardens, keep a cow, care for poultry, pigs etc At Snow Hill Alabama the Negro demonstrators have formed a club and agreed on "a standard," requiring every member to possess an enclosed garden, "in which something must be kept growing the year round," to keep at least one hog for each member of the family, not less than 30 hens, and a cow or two, to preserve or can fruit sufficient for the family's demand, to plant shrubs and whitewash the house, and to take at least one agricultural paper Local agents report many instances of improved farm equipments due to demonstration work, home gardens, wire fences new mules harvesters, riding cultivators, grain drills, enlarged houses, cleaned premises and the liberal use of whitewash   The farm demonstration arouses pride and stimulates energy   The net outcome has never been more picturesquely summed up than by a Negro farmer in Virginia   "You done turned the river down and waked us up '

The General Education Board has also undertaken a special work among the Negroes to improve Negro rural schools under the idea that it is the rural school that is the thing of special interest for Negro improvement since 80 per cent of the Negroes in the Southern States live on the farm   Beginning on page 194 we read as follows

STATE SUPERVISORS OF NEGRO RURAL SCHOOLS

For the purpose of arousing interest in furnishing intelligent and specialized guidance, a State supervisor of Negro schools was supported in Virginia by the Peabody Educational Fund and the Southern Educational Board   The appointee had already demonstrated the value of such supervision while superintendent of schools in Henico County, Virginia   The General Education Board, recognizing the importance of this work, decided to extend it throughout the South as opportunity occurred   The board offered to co-operate with the State Department of Education by furnishing funds adequate to pay the salaries and expenses of State agents for Negro rural schools   Appropriations were to be made to State Department and only on application of these departments, the agent, or supervisor, as he is usually called, was to be chosen by the State Superintendent of Education and thus become a State official with all the powers and responsibilities of such a position   On this basis agents are now supported by the General Education Board in the States of Alabama, Arkansas, Georgia, Kentucky, North Carolina, Tennessee and Virginia

These agents are white men who have had large and successful experience in school management   They have in every instance gained the confidence not only of the colored people and the public school authorities, but of the white citizens in general   As representing the State Department they have the entire to all counties, communities and schools, they transact the State's business with county superintendents, county school boards, local trustees and teachers   They interest the Negroes of a vicinity in the local school and bring the two races to join in its improvement   Substantial sums have been obtained from both races for local school improvement   They have already brought about the consolidation of several weak schools into central schools, they have participated in planning and constructing school buildings, in choosing teachers, in improving the curriculum, especially along industrial and domestic lines, in effecting co-operation between the schools, farm demonstration and club agents, and in securing gradually increasing allotments from public funds, of which, however, the expenditure on the Negro is still disproportionately small   For the support of these agents the General Education Board appropriates $2,500 each per year for salary and a sum of not to exceed $1,000 each for necessary expenses

CO-OPERATION WITH THE ANNA T JEANES FUND

The effectiveness of this work has been greatly increased by its intimate association with the activities of the industrial supervisors and teachers supported by the Jeanes' fund   These teachers, appointed by the county superintendents and working under their direction, are at the same time in close co-operation with the State agent maintained by the General Education Board   At the present time 128 such teachers are at work   They are for the most part graduates of Hampton, Tuskegee, Petersburg, Fisk, Atlanta, Spelman and kindred institutions   Each teacher visits a number of county schools, gives a lesson in some industry, plans with the regular teacher to give additional lessons in her absence, organizes parents' clubs, and starts a movement for better school equipment or longer term, counsels the local teacher about her daily teaching, and stirs the community to united efforts to better the school   Many of these teachers are employed for the entire year, when school is no longer in session, they carry on similar work in the community   Wherever the industrial teacher and the rural school supervisor have gone, quick improvement is perceptible in the physical appearance of grounds, buildings and pupils   Improvement leagues are formed, money is raised by subscription to paint or whitewash the building, to buy a stove and procure the necessary equipment for cooking classes both among the girls and their mothers   Elementary sanitation is inculcated, fans and exhibitions are held through which the results are brought together for the pleasure and enlightenment of the pupils and patrons   In 1912-13, 23 supervising teachers worked under the general direction of the State supervisors in 25 Virginia counties, 591 schools were visited, 417 of them regularly, 189 extended their term by one month, their patrons bearing the expense, 20 new school houses were built at a cost of $23,808, 15 more were enlarged at a cost of $2 212, 428 school leagues raised among Negroes $22,655

In 1913-14, supervising industrial teachers worked in 27 counties, 22 new Negro school houses, costing $18,230, were built, 12 enlarged at a cost of $3,612, 182 extended their terms one month through subscriptions, mainly of their patrons, 125 sanitary outhouses were built, $28,673 was raised by Negroes for school improvements

ACCOMPLISHMENTS IN VIRGINIA

It is impossible to draw a sharp line between this work and that of the clubs described as part of the farm denominations   In Virginia, for example, 14 teachers report 617 girls in clubs of fifteen counties with 416 home gardens of which two-thirds are "excellent"   The girls put up 10,504 jars of vegetables for home use, their mothers 12,269   "I spent August 5 and 6 with Superintendent Washington of Caroline County,' writes the State Supervisor in September, 1913

"We joined the supervising teacher and the special agent in charge of canning clubs, and drove through the country, visiting the gardens of the various members of the club Every garden was laid off in straight rows, usually eight, with a walk in the middle   There were two rows of flowers, two rows of cabbage, two rows of snap beans, one early and one late, and two rows of tomatoes   They were well cultivated and most of them had resisted the temptation to 'hill' the tomatoes, and cultivate level, as they were directed In nearly every case the tomatoes were held up by some support "

On the 8th there was held at Bowling Green the first conference of girls' canning and poultry clubs of Caroline County   Nearly all of the eight members were present with their parents and other members of their families   They brought exhibits of their vegetables, canned goods, bread, cake, sewing, poultry, etc   Simple prizes given by the County School Board were awarded   Girls who had been most successful and those who had overcome unusual difficulties were called on to tell how they cultivated their gardens, how they made their fences, how they canned their tomatoes or baked bread   The prize for the best kept garden was awarded to two motherless girls, 11 and 12 years of age, who kept house for their father   Their garden, located in a piece of newly cleared land, was a model of neatness and careful cultivation   Similar experiences can be reported from the other States

IMPROVED RELATIONS OF THE RACES

A more cordial relation between the races has followed in the wake of educational progress   Nothing, indeed, is of fairer promise than the awakened interest of the white —superintendents and laymen—in the improvement of Negro schools   For example, a conference of Alabama county superintendents with the State superintendent and the State supervisor of Negro schools, visits Tuskegee Institute in a body and confesses "a new vision in regard to the Negro"   Again, the State supervisor addresses the Young Men's Christian Association of the State College of Agriculture at Auburn Ala, on the Negro problem, and 45 members subsequently accompanied him on a visit of inspection to Tuskegee   At one of the summer institutes held for Negro teachers in Georgia the work of the Negro industrial teacher was so novel and interesting that the white county superintendent asked her to come over to the white institute in order to give a demonstration of her work   She was kept half a day answering questions and explaining the way she did the work   At other times, white teachers have gone to see what the Negroes were doing in their institutes   What they observe surprises the whites and the experience affords pleasure and stimulation to the Negro teachers   "Shall this not be a mighty entering wedge to reach the prejudice and sympathy of the white people?" asks the State agent in reporting the incidents   From North Carolina comes an account of a meeting of leading white citizens at the Slater Normal School for Negroes Among them were the city and county superintendents of schools and several members of the board of trustees   The object of the meeting was to study the conditions and needs of the normal schools in order to devise means by which it may train more and better teachers and serve the Negro race more effectively   Plans for the erection of a new dormitory for girls and for improving the teacher training course were discussed "

THE CAPABILITY OF THE NEGRO RACE

Can any one doubt the capability of the Negroes to respond to modern industrial cultural methods? Our past achievements as Negroes are such as to awaken new confidence in ourselves and new hope and determination for the future   We constitute a population of 9,827,763, or 10 7 per cent of the total population in 1910   Only 47 3 per cent of the Negro school population of 6 to 20 years, inclusive, enjoy school advantages as compared to 66 9 per cent of the whites, and yet, with an average school attendance of only about three months in the year, we have reduced our illiteracy since 1865 from 100 per cent to 30 4 per cent   In 1910 Southern Negroes owned 1,917,391 homes, an increase in home owning over 1900 of 2 4 per cent   Of the total number of Negroes over 10 years of age, namely 7,317,292, 71 per cent, or 5,192,535, were engaged in self-supporting labor   The total number of farms in the United States in 1910 was 6,261 500, of which Negroes operated 893,370, representing a total value in investment of $1,142,000,000 Three-fourths of the Negro farmers were tenants and one-fourth were owners   Perhaps the most remarkable of all the revelations of the census of 1910 is the fact that the death rate of the Negroes showed a decrease of 3 9 per cent , although the death rate of the Negroes is still almost twice as high as that of the whites, showing there is yet a vast work of reform in hygiene and sanitation to be achieved among Negroes

Teachers of my race, let us gird our loins anew and put on the whole armor of righteousness and efficiency   Let us study anew the problems of education,   that wonderful process which as being a characteristic of living beings is in reality as indefinable as life itself   But by its fruits we can know, define and direct it   And who can doubt that it is in all races and under all its names and guises eventually a moral process, a development of character, of essential manhood and womanhood   In these days the slogan of all efforts is service and the good of education is thus a moral one—service to our fellowmen and "as ye would that men should do to you do ye even so to them," said the Great Teacher, who also said He came not to be ministered unto but to minister unto others and who girded His loins and washed His disciples' feet, and who declared on one occasion   "He that would be greatest among you, let him be servant of all "   He gave His life for man   and in His name and baptized in His spirit let us give our lives to the children of our race, in the spirit of Him who loved little children and said   "Suffer little children to come unto me, and forbid them not for of such is the kingdom of heaven "

Let us as teachers of a race inculcate the spirit of friendliness toward the white race and, indeed, toward all races of men   Nothing is so potent as love and loving kindness and love is the great solvent of all problems as it is also the fulfilling of the law of our being   The world is in the throes of a worldwide war, but by and by peace will come and will encircle the globe as an earnest of the greater and more enduring peace of Christ between all races of men which the choral angels once sang about to awestruck shepherds above Judea's moonlit plains   "Glory to God in the highest and on earth peace, good will toward men "

CONTENTS

PAGE

INTRODUCTORY   3

FRONTISPIECE   4
A Few Harris County Survivors of Ante-Bellum Days.

EFFICIENCY   5
By Emmett J. Scott.

VIEW OF COLORED CARNEGIE LIBRARY   12

VIEW OF HOUSTON INDUSTRIAL COLLEGE   12

HOUSTON COLLEGE SETTLEMENT ASSOCIATION....   12

COLORED SCHOOLS OF HOUSTON   13
By Prof. E. O. Smith.

PROGRESS OF NEGRO CHURCHES IN HOUSTON SINCE EMANCIPATION OR THE CIVIL WAR.   21
By Rev. W. H. Logan.

BRIEF SKETCH OF HOUSTON BAPTISTS..   24
By F. L. Lights, D. D.

INDUSTRIAL LIFE IN THE UNITED STATES.   26

PHOTOS AND VIEWS OF CHURCHES.......   31

COLORED METHODIST EPISCOPAL CHURCH   53

PHOTOS.   55

RISE OF THE RACE   61

VIEWS OF CHURCHES AND PHOTOS.....   69

HOUSTON CHURCHES   72

PAUL QUINN COLLEGE, WACO, TEXAS.......   78

THE FULLNESS OF TIME (a Poem)..   79

VIEWS OF HOUSTON SCHOOLS.......   87

SCHOOLS AND TEACHERS   91

CLUBS AND LODGES...   96

VIEWS OF RESIDENCES AND PHOTOS.   99

SOCIAL CALENDAR.....   108

PHOTOS AND VIEWS OF RESIDENCES...   112

MARKS OF PROGRESS   116

CHURCH ORGANIZATIONS AND PASTORS   120

VIEWS OF RESIDENCES AND PHOTOS   122

AN ADDRESS AT EMANCIPATION CELEBRATION IN HOUSTON   126
By Hon. W. M. C. Dickson.

PHOTOS AND VIEWS OF RESIDENCES   130

DIGEST OF RULES OF ETIQUETTE   138

PHOTOS .   141

NEGRO HEALTH PROBLEM   148
By Dr. H. E. Lee.

PROFESSIONAL AND INDUSTRIAL LIST   152

CLASSIFIED BUSINESS, PROFESSIONAL AND INDUSTRIAL LIST............   164

PRAIRIE VIEW NORMAL AND INDUSTRIAL COLLEGE, PRAIRIE VIEW, TEXAS ..   175

CPSIA information can be obtained
at www.ICGtesting.com
Printed in the USA
LVHW082159230120
644669LV00007B/429